STAR WARS®

A NEW HOPE

SCRIPT FACSIMILE

PUBLISHED BY DEL REY BOOKS:

Art of Star Wars: A New Hope

Art of Star Wars: The Empire Strikes Back

Art of Star Wars: Return of the Jedi

Star Wars: A New Hope
The National Public Radio Dramatization

Star Wars: The Empire Strikes Back
The National Public Radio Dramatization

Star Wars: Return of the Jedi
The National Public Radio Dramatization

Star Wars: The Annotated Screenplays

A Guide to the Star Wars Universe

Star Wars Encyclopedia

Star Wars: A New Hope
The Illustrated Screenplay

Star Wars: The Empire Strikes Back
The Illustrated Screenplay

Star Wars: Return of the Jedi
The Illustrated Screenplay

A NEW HOPE

SCRIPT FACSIMILE

GEORGE LUCAS

THE BALLANTINE PUBLISHING GROUP

NEW YORK

A Del Rey® Book
Published by The Ballantine Publishing Group

Star Wars® and copyright © 1997, 1998 by Lucasfilm Ltd. Title and character and place names protected by all applicable trademark laws. Copyright © 1979 by Star Wars Corporation. All Rights Reserved. Used Under Authorization.

All rights reserved under International and Pan-American Copyright Conventions. Published in the United States by The Ballantine Publishing Group, a division of Random House, Inc., New York, and simultaneously in Canada by Random House of Canada Limited, Toronto. Originally published in different form in *Star Wars: A New Hope Illustrated Screenplay* and *Star Wars: The Annotated Screenplays*.

http://www.randomhouse.com/delrey/

Library of Congress Catalog Card Number: 98-96426

ISBN 0-345-42080-2

Cover design by Min Choi

Manufactured in the United States of America

First Edition: November 1998

10 9 8 7 6 5 4 3 2 1

Dear Reader:

In 1997 Lucasfilm Ltd. released all three of
the original <u>Star Wars</u> films as the <u>Star Wars</u>
<u>Trilogy Special Edition</u>. Filmmaker George Lucas
was afforded the extraordinary opportunity to
complete these landmark films as he had
originally envisioned them, and to restore each
to the highest visual and sound quality
available.

With the Special Edition releases, Lucas was
able to take advantage of two decades of
advances in filmmaking technology that had begun
with the original <u>Star Wars: A New Hope</u> and had
been spearheaded by the special effects wizards
of Industrial Light & Magic. And in doing so,
he was able to get the ball rolling on
advancements that very likely play a major role
in the next <u>Star Wars</u> trilogy, beginning with
<u>Episode I</u> in 1999.

Before the Special Edition trilogy could be
executed, the Lucasfilm creative team had to
work closely with Lucas to identify each scene
that would be created or recovered, each
special effect that would be added or improved
upon. Then they had to fit each scene into the
original film, so the result would flow
seamlessly across the theater screen.

What you hold in your hands is a first: the
original movie script, with the Special Edition
scene descriptions inserted. This script
represents the complete screenplay. As a bonus,
you also have a photo gallery that shows some
of the end results, including photo stills that
are being published for the very first time.

We hope you enjoy this book as much as we
enjoyed having a part in its creation.

The Editors:
Sue Rostoni
Steve Saffel

A long time ago in a galaxy far, far
away . . . .

A vast sea of stars serves as the backdrop for the main
title. War drums echo through the heavens as a roll-up
slowly crawls into infinity.

It is a period of civil war. Rebel space-
ships, striking from a hidden base, have won
their first victory against the evil Galactic
Empire.

During the battle, Rebel spies managed to
steal secret plans to the Empire's ultimate
weapon, the Death Star, an armored space
station with enough power to destroy an
entire planet.

Pursued by the Empire's sinister agents,
Princess Leia races home aboard her starship,
custodian of the stolen plans that can save
her people and restore freedom to the
galaxy . . .

CONTINUED:

The awesome yellow planet of Tatooine emerges from a total eclipse,
her two moons glowing against the darkness. A tiny silver spacecraft, a Rebel Blockade Runner firing lasers from the back of the
ship, races through space. It is pursued by a giant Imperial
starship. Hundreds of deadly laserbolts streak from the Imperial
Star Destroyer, causing the main solar fin of the Rebel craft to
disintegrate.

INT. REBEL BLOCKADE RUNNER — MAIN PASSAGEWAY

An explosion rocks the ship as two robots, Artoo-Detoo (R2-D2) and
See-Threepio (C-3PO) struggle to make their way through the shaking,
bouncing passageway. Both robots are old and battered. Artoo is a
short, claw-armed tripod. His face is a mass of computer lights
surrounding a radar eye. Threepio, on the other hand, is a tall,
slender robot of human proportions. He has a gleaming bronze-like
metallic surface of an Art Deco design.

Another blast shakes them as they struggle along their way.

                    THREEPIO
          Did you hear that? They've shut down the main
          reactor. We'll be destroyed for sure. This is
          madness!

Rebel troopers rush past the robots and take up positions in the
main passageway. They aim their weapons toward the door.

                    THREEPIO
          We're doomed!

The little R2 unit makes a series of electronic sounds that only
another robot could understand.

                    THREEPIO
          There'll be no escape for the princess this
          time.

Artoo continues making beeping sounds. Tension mounts as loud
metallic latches clank and the screams of heavy equipment are heard
moving around the outside hull of the ship.

                    THREEPIO
          What's that?

EXT. SPACECRAFT IN SPACE

The Imperial craft has easily overtaken the Rebel Blockade Runner.
The smaller Rebel ship is being drawn into the underside dock of the
giant Imperial starship.

INT. REBEL BLOCKADE RUNNER

The nervous Rebel troopers aim their weapons. Suddenly a tremendous
blast opens up a hole in the main passageway and a score of fearsome
armored spacesuited stormtroopers make their way into the smoke-
filled corridor.

In a few minutes the entire passageway is ablaze with laserfire. The
deadly bolts ricochet in wild random patterns creating huge explosions. Stormtroopers scatter and duck behind storage lockers. Laserbolts hit several Rebel soldiers who scream and stagger through the
smoke, holding shattered arms and faces.

An explosion hits near the robots.

                    THREEPIO
          I should have known better than to trust the
          logic of a half-sized thermocapsulary dehous-
          ing assister . . .

Artoo counters with an angry rebuttal as the battle rages around the
two hapless robots.

EXT. TATOOINE — DESERT WASTELAND — DAY

A death-white wasteland stretches from horizon to horizon. The
tremendous heat of two huge twin suns settles on a lone figure, Luke
Skywalker, a farm boy with heroic aspirations who looks much younger
than his eighteen years. His shaggy hair and baggy tunic give him
the air of a simple but lovable lad with a prize-winning smile.

A light wind whips at him as he adjusts several valves on a large
battered moisture vaporator which sticks out of the desert floor
much like an oil pipe with valves. He is aided by a beat-up tread-
robot with six claw arms. The little robot appears to be barely
functioning and moves with jerky motions. A bright sparkle in the
morning sky catches Luke's eye and he instinctively grabs a pair of
electrobinoculars from his utility belt. He stands transfixed for a
few moments studying the heavens, then dashes toward his dented,
crudely repaired landspeeder (an auto-like transport that travels a
few feet above the ground on a magnetic field). He motions for the
tiny robot to follow him.

                    LUKE
          Hurry up! Come with me! What are you waiting
          for?! Get in gear!

The robot scoots around in a tight circle, stops short, and smoke
begins to pour out of every joint. Luke throws his arms up in
disgust. Exasperated, the young farm boy jumps into his landspeeder
leaving the smoldering robot to hum madly.

INT. REBEL BLOCKADE RUNNER — MAIN HALLWAY

The awesome, seven-foot-tall Dark Lord of the Sith makes his way
into the blinding light of the main passageway. This is Darth Vader,
right hand of the Emperor. His face is obscured by his flowing black
robes and grotesque breath mask, which stands out next to the
fascist white armored suits of the Imperial stormtroopers. Everyone
instinctively backs away from the imposing warrior and a deathly
quiet sweeps through the Rebel troops. Several of the Rebel troops
break and run in a frenzied panic.

INT. REBEL BLOCKADE RUNNER

A woman's hand puts a card into an opening in Artoo's dome. Artoo
makes beeping sounds.

INT. REBEL BLOCKADE RUNNER

Threepio stands in a hallway, somewhat bewildered. Artoo is nowhere
in sight. The pitiful screams of the doomed Rebel soldiers can be
heard in the distance.

                    THREEPIO
          Artoo! Artoo-Detoo, where are you?

A familiar clanking sound attracts Threepio's attention and he spots
little Artoo at the end of the hallway in a smoke-filled alcove. A
beautiful young girl (about sixteen years old) stands in front of
Artoo. Surreal and out of place, dreamlike and half hidden in the
smoke, she finishes adjusting something on Artoo's computer face,
then watches as the little robot joins his companion.

                    THREEPIO
          At last! Where have you been?

Stormtroopers can be heard battling in the distance.

                    THREEPIO
          They're heading in this direction. What
          are we going to do? We'll be sent to the
          spice mines of Kessel or smashed into
          who-knows-what!

Artoo scoots past his bronze friend and races down the subhallway.
Threepio chases after him.

                    THREEPIO
          Wait a minute, where are you going?

Artoo responds with electronic beeps.

INT. REBEL BLOCKADE RUNNER — CORRIDOR

The evil Darth Vader stands amid the broken and twisted bodies of
his foes. He grabs a wounded Rebel Officer by the neck as an
Imperial Officer rushes up to the Dark Lord.

                    IMPERIAL OFFICER
          The Death Star plans are not in the main
          computer.

Vader squeezes the neck of the Rebel Officer, who struggles in vain.

                    VADER
          Where are those transmissions you
          intercepted?

Vader lifts the Rebel off his feet by his throat.

                    VADER
          What have you done with those plans?

                    REBEL OFFICER
          We intercepted no transmissions. Aaah . . .
          This is a consular ship. We're on a diplo-
          matic mission.

                    VADER
          If this is a consular ship . . . where is the
          Ambassador?

The Rebel refuses to speak but eventually cries out as the Dark Lord
begins to squeeze the officer's throat, creating a gruesome snapping
and choking, until the soldier goes limp. Vader tosses the dead
soldier against the wall and turns to his troops.

                    VADER
          Commander, tear this ship apart until you've
          found those plans and bring me the Ambas-
          sador. I want her alive!

The stormtroopers scurry into the subhallways.

INT. REBEL BLOCKADE RUNNER — SUBHALLWAY

The lovely young girl huddles in a small alcove as the stormtroopers
search through the ship. She is Princess Leia Organa, a member of
the Alderaan Senate. The fear in her eyes slowly gives way to anger
as the muted crushing sounds of the approaching stormtroopers grow
louder. One of the troopers spots her.

                    TROOPER
          There she is! Set for stun!

Leia steps from her hiding place and blasts a trooper with her laser

                                                  (CONTINUED)

CONTINUED:

pistol. She starts to run but is felled by a paralyzing ray. The
troopers inspect her inert body.

> TROOPER
> She'll be all right. Inform Lord Vader we
> have a prisoner.

INT. REBEL BLOCKADE RUNNER — SUBHALLWAY

Artoo stops before the small hatch of an emergency lifepod. He snaps
the seal on the main latch and a red warning light begins to flash.
The stubby astro-robot works his way into the cramped four-man pod.

> THREEPIO
> Hey, you're not permitted in there. It's
> restricted. You'll be deactivated for sure.

Artoo beeps something to him.

> THREEPIO
> Don't call me a mindless philosopher, you
> overweight glob of grease! Now come out
> before somebody sees you.

Artoo whistles something at his reluctant friend regarding the
mission he is about to perform.

> THREEPIO
> Secret mission? What plans? What are you
> talking about? I'm not getting in there!

Artoo isn't happy with Threepio's stubbornness, and he beeps and
twangs angrily.

A new explosion, this time very close, sends dust and debris through
the narrow subhallway. Flames lick at Threepio and, after a flurry
of electronic swearing from Artoo, the lanky robot jumps into the
lifepod.

> THREEPIO
> I'm going to regret this.

EXT. REBEL BLOCKADE RUNNER

The safety door snaps shut, and with the thunder of exploding
latches the tiny lifepod ejects from the disabled ship.

INT. IMPERIAL STAR DESTROYER

On the main viewscreen, the lifepod carrying the two terrified
robots speeds away from the stricken Rebel spacecraft.

CONTINUED:

                  CHIEF PILOT
        There goes another one.

                  CAPTAIN
        Hold your fire. There are no life forms. It
        must have been short-circuited.

INT. LIFEPOD

Artoo and Threepio look out at the receding Imperial starship. Stars circle as the pod rotates through the galaxy.

                  THREEPIO
        That's funny, the damage doesn't look as bad
        from out here.

Artoo beeps an assuring response.

                  THREEPIO
        Are you sure this thing is safe?

EXT. TATOOINE — ANCHORHEAD SETTLEMENT — POWER
STATION — DAY

Heat waves radiate from the dozen or so bleached white buildings. Luke pilots his landspeeder through the dusty empty street of the tiny settlement. An old woman runs to get out of the way of the speeding vehicle, shaking her fist at Luke as he flies past.

                  WOMAN
        I've told you kids to slow down!

Luke pulls up behind a low concrete service station that is all but covered by the shifting desert sands.

INT. POWER STATION — DAY

Luke bursts into the power station, waking The Fixer, a rugged mechanic and Camie, a sexy, disheveled girl who has been asleep on his lap. They grumble as he races through the office, yelling wildly.

                  FIXER
        Did I hear a young noise blast through here?

                  CAMIE
        It was just Wormie on another rampage.

Luke bounces into a small room behind the office where Deak and Windy, two tough boys about the same age as Luke, are playing a computer pool-like game with Biggs, a burly, handsome boy a few

                                  (CONTINUED)

CONTINUED:

years older than the rest. His flashy city attire is a sharp
contrast to the loose-fitting tunics of the farm boys. A robot
repairs some equipment in the background.

                         LUKE
          Shape it up you guys! . . . Biggs?

Luke's surprise at the appearance of Biggs gives way to great joy
and emotion. They give each other a great bear hug.

                         LUKE
          I didn't know you were back! When did you
          get in?

                         BIGGS
          Just now. I wanted to surprise you, hot shot.
          I thought you'd be here . . . certainly
          didn't expect you to be out working. (he
          laughs)

                         LUKE
          The Academy didn't change you much . . . but
          you're back so soon? Hey, what happened,
          didn't you get your commission?

Biggs has an air of cool that seems slightly phony.

                         BIGGS
          Of course I got it. Signed aboard the Rand
          Ecliptic last week. First mate Biggs
          Darklighter at your service . . . (he
          salutes) . . . I just came back to say
          good-bye to all you unfortunate landlocked
          simpletons.

Everyone laughs. The dazzling spectacle of his dashing friend is
almost too much for Luke, but suddenly he snaps out of it.

                         LUKE
          I almost forgot. There's a battle going on!
          Right here in our system. Come and look!

                         DEAK
          Not again! Forget it.

EXT. TATOOINE — ANCHORHEAD SETTLEMENT — POWER STATION — DAY

The group stumbles out into the stifling desert sun. Camie and The
Fixer complain and are forced to shade their eyes. Luke has his
electrobinoculars out scanning the heavens.

                         LUKE
          There they are!

                                                   (CONTINUED)

CONTINUED:

Biggs takes the electrobinoculars from Luke as the others strain to
see something with the naked eye. Through the electrobinoculars
Biggs sees two small silver specks.

                    BIGGS
          That's no battle, hot shot . . . they're just
          sitting there! Probably a freighter-tanker
          refueling.

                    LUKE
          But there was a lot of firing earlier . . .

Camie grabs the electrobinoculars away banging them against the
building in the process. Luke grabs them.

                    LUKE
          Hey, easy with those . . .

                    CAMIE
          Don't worry about it, Wormie.

The Fixer gives Luke a hard look and the young farm boy shrugs his
shoulders in resignation.

                    FIXER
          I keep telling you, the Rebellion is a long
          way from here. I doubt if the Empire would
          even fight to keep this system. Believe me
          Luke, this planet is a big hunk of
          nothing . . .

Luke agrees, although it's obvious he isn't sure why. The group
stumbles back into the power station, grumbling about Luke's
ineptitude.

INT. REBEL BLOCKADE RUNNER — HALLWAY

Princess Leia is led down a low-ceilinged hallway by a squad of
armored stormtroopers. Her hands are bound and she is brutally
shoved when she is unable to keep up with the briskly marching
troops. They stop in a smoky hallway as Darth Vader emerges from the
shadows. The sinister Dark Lord stares hard at the frail young
senator, but she doesn't move.

                    LEIA
          Lord Vader, I should have known. Only you
          could be so bold. The Imperial Senate will
          not sit still for this, when they hear you've
          attacked a diplomatic . . .

                    VADER
          Don't play games with me, Your Highness. You
          weren't on any mercy mission this time. You
                    (MORE)

                                              (CONTINUED)

CONTINUED:

                    VADER (CONT'D)
         passed directly through a restricted system.
         Several transmissions were beamed to this
         ship by Rebel spies. I want to know what
         happened to the plans they sent you.

                    LEIA
         I don't know what you're talking about. I'm a
         member of the Imperial Senate on a diplomatic
         mission to Alderaan . . .

                    VADER
         You're a part of the Rebel Alliance . . . and
         a traitor. Take her away!

Leia is marched away down the hallway and into the smoldering hole
blasted in the side of the ship. An Imperial Commander turns to
Vader.

                    COMMANDER
         Holding her is dangerous. If word of this
         gets out, it could generate sympathy for the
         Rebellion in the senate.

                    VADER
         I have traced the Rebel spies to her. Now she
         is my only link to finding their secret base!

                    COMMANDER
         She'll die before she'll tell you anything.

                    VADER
         Leave that to me. Send a distress signal and
         then inform the senate that all aboard were
         killed!

Another Imperial Officer approaches Vader and the Commander. They
stop and snap to attention.

                    SECOND OFFICER
         Lord Vader, the battle station plans are not
         aboard this ship! And no transmissions were
         made. An escape pod was jettisoned during the
         fighting, but no life forms were aboard.

Vader turns to the commander.

                    VADER
         She must have hidden the plans in the escape
         pod. Send a detachment down to retrieve them.
         See to it personally, Commander. There'll be
         no one to stop us this time.

                    SECOND OFFICER
         Yes, sir.

EXT. SPACE

The Imperial Star Destroyer comes over the surface of the planet Tatooine.

EXT. TATOOINE — DESERT

Jundland, or "No Man's Land," where the rugged desert mesas meet the foreboding Dune Sea. The two helpless astro-robots kick up clouds of sand as they leave the lifepod and clumsily work their way across the desert wasteland. The lifepod in the distance rests half buried in the sand.

> THREEPIO
> How did we get into this mess? I really don't
> know how. We seem to be made to suffer. It's
> our lot in life.

Artoo answers with beeping sounds.

> THREEPIO
> I've got to rest before I fall apart. My
> joints are almost frozen.

Artoo continues to respond with beeping sounds.

> THREEPIO
> What a desolate place this is.

Suddenly Artoo whistles, makes a sharp right turn and starts off in the direction of the rocky desert mesas. Threepio stops and yells at him.

> THREEPIO
> Where are you going?

A stream of electronic noises pours forth from the small robot.

> THREEPIO
> Well, I'm not going that way. It's much too
> rocky. This way is much easier.

Artoo counters with a long whistle.

> THREEPIO
> What makes you think there are settlements
> over there?

Artoo continues to make beeping sounds.

> THREEPIO
> Don't get technical with me.

Artoo continues to make beeping sounds.

(CONTINUED)

CONTINUED:

                        THREEPIO
        What mission? What are you talking about?
        I've had just about enough of you! Go that
        way! You'll be malfunctioning within a day,
        you nearsighted scrap pile!

Threepio gives the little robot a kick and starts off in the direction of the vast Dune Sea.

                        THREEPIO
        And don't let me catch you following me
        begging for help, because you won't get it.

Artoo's reply is a rather rude sound. He turns and trudges off in
the direction of the towering mesas.

                        THREEPIO
        No more adventures. I'm not going that way.

Artoo beeps to himself as he makes his way toward the distant
mountains.

EXT. TATOOINE — DUNE SEA

Threepio, hot and tired, struggles up over the ridge of a dune; only
to find more dunes, which seem to go on for endless miles. He looks
back in the direction of the now distant rock mesas.

                        THREEPIO
        That malfunctioning little twerp. This is all
        his fault! He tricked me into going this way,
        but he'll do no better.

In a huff of anger and frustration, Threepio knocks the sand from
his joints. His plight seems hopeless, when a glint of reflected
light in the distance reveals an object moving toward him.

                        THREEPIO
        Wait, what's that? A transport! I'm saved!

The bronze droid waves frantically and yells at the approaching
transport.

                        THREEPIO
        Over here! Help! Please, help!

EXT. TATOOINE — ANCHORHEAD SETTLEMENT — POWER
STATION — DAY

Luke and Biggs are walking and drinking a malt brew. Fixer and the
others can be heard working inside.

                                              (CONTINUED)

CONTINUED:

                         LUKE
          (very animated) . . . so I cut off my power,
          shut down the afterburners and came in low on
          Deak's trail. I was so close I thought I was
          going to fry my instruments. As it was I
          busted up the skyhopper pretty bad. Uncle
          Owen was pretty upset. He grounded me for the
          rest of the season. You should have been
          there . . . it was fantastic.

                         BIGGS
          You ought to take it a little easy, Luke. You
          may be the hottest bushpilot this side of Mos
          Eisley, but those little skyhoppers are
          dangerous. Keep it up, and one day, whammo,
          you're going to be nothing more than a dark
          spot on the down side of a canyon wall.

                         LUKE
          Look who's talking. Now that you've been
          around those giant starships you're beginning
          to sound like my uncle. You've gotten soft in
          the city . . .

                         BIGGS
          I've missed you, kid.

                         LUKE
          Well, things haven't been the same since you
          left, Biggs. It's been so . . . quiet.

Biggs looks around then leans close to Luke.

                         BIGGS
          Luke, I didn't come back just to say good-
          bye . . . I shouldn't tell you this, but
          you're the only one I can trust . . . and if
          I don't come back, I want somebody to know.

Luke's eyes are wide with Biggs's seriousness and loyalty.

                         LUKE
          What are you talking about?

                         BIGGS
          I made some friends at the Academy (he
          whispers) . . . when our frigate goes to one
          of the central systems, we're going to jump
          ship and join the Alliance . . .

Luke, amazed and stunned, is almost speechless.

                         LUKE
          Join the Rebellion?! Are you kidding! How?

CONTINUED:

                              BIGGS
            Quiet down will ya! You got a mouth bigger
            than a meteor crater!

                              LUKE
            I'm sorry. I'm quiet. (he whispers) Listen
            how quiet I am. You can barely hear me . . .

Biggs shakes his head angrily and then continues.

                              BIGGS
            My friend has a friend on Bestine who might
            help us make contact.

                              LUKE
            You're crazy! You could wander around forever
            trying to find them.

                              BIGGS
            I know it's a long shot, but if I don't find
            them I'll do what I can on my own . . . It's
            what we always talked about. Luke, I'm not
            going to wait for the Empire to draft me into
            service. The Rebellion is spreading and I
            want to be on the right side — the side I
            believe in.

                              LUKE
            And I'm stuck here . . .

                              BIGGS
            I thought you were going to the Academy next
            term. You'll get your chance to get off this
            rock.

                              LUKE
            Not likely! I had to cancel my application.
            There has been a lot of unrest among the Sand
            People since you left . . . they've even
            raided the outskirts of Anchorhead.

                              BIGGS
            Your uncle could hold off a whole colony of
            Sand People with one blaster.

                              LUKE
            I know, but he's got enough vaporators going
            to make the place pay off. He needs me for
            just one more season. I can't leave him now.

                              BIGGS
            I feel for you, Luke, you're going to have to
            learn what seems to be important or what
            really is important. What good is all your
                            (MORE)

                                              (CONTINUED)

CONTINUED:

                    BIGGS(CONT'D)
uncle's work if it's taken over by the
Empire? . . . You know they're starting to
nationalize commerce in the central systems
. . . It won't be long before your uncle is
merely a tenant, slaving for the greater
glory of the Empire.

                    LUKE
It couldn't happen here. You said it
yourself. The Empire won't bother with this
rock.

                    BIGGS
Things always change.

                    LUKE
I wish I was going . . . Are you going to be
around long?

                    BIGGS
No, I'm leaving in the morning . . .

                    LUKE
Then I guess I won't see you.

                    BIGGS
Maybe someday . . . I'll keep a lookout.

                    LUKE
Well, I'll be at the Academy next
season . . . after that who knows. I won't be
drafted into the Imperial Starfleet that's
for sure . . . Take care of yourself, you'll
always be the best friend I've got.

                    BIGGS
So long, Luke.

Biggs turns away from his old friend and heads back towards the
power station.

EXT. TATOOINE — ROCK CANYON — SUNSET

The gargantuan rock formations are shrouded in a strange foreboding
mist and the ominous sounds of unearthly creatures fill the air.
Artoo moves cautiously through the creepy rock canyon, inadvertently
making a loud clicking noise as he goes. He hears a distant, hard,
metallic sound and stops for a moment. Convinced he is alone, he
continues on his way.

In the distance, a pebble tumbles down the steep canyon wall and a
small dark figure darts into the shadows. A little further up the

                                                      (CONTINUED)

CONTINUED:

canyon a slight flicker of light reveals a pair of eyes in the dark recesses only a few feet from the narrow path.

The unsuspecting robot waddles along the rugged trail until suddenly, out of nowhere, a powerful magnetic ray shoots out of the rocks and engulfs him in an eerie glow. He manages one short electronic squeak before he topples over onto his back. His bright computer lights flicker off, then on, then off again. Out of the rocks scurry three Jawas, no taller than Artoo. They holster strange and complex weapons as they cautiously approach the robot. They wear grubby cloaks and their faces are shrouded so that only their glowing yellow eyes can be seen. They hiss and make odd guttural sounds as they heave the heavy robot onto their shoulders and carry him off down the trail.

EXT. TATOOINE — ROCK CANYON — SANDCRAWLER — SUNSET

The eight Jawas carry Artoo out of the canyon to a huge tank-like vehicle the size of a four-story house. They weld a small disk on the side of Artoo and then put him under a large tube on the side of the vehicle and the little robot is sucked into the giant machine.

The filthy little Jawas scurry like rats up small ladders and enter the main cabin of the behemoth transport.

INT. SANDCRAWLER — HOLD AREA

It is dim inside the hold area of the sandcrawler. Artoo switches on a small floodlight on his forehead and stumbles around the scrap heap. The narrow beam swings across rusty metal rocket parts and an array of grotesquely twisted and maimed astro-robots. He lets out a pathetic electronic whimper and stumbles off toward what appears to be a door at the end of the chamber.

INT. SANDCRAWLER — PRISON AREA

Artoo enters a wide room with a four-foot ceiling. In the middle of the scrap heap sit a dozen or so robots of various shapes and sizes. Some are engaged in electronic conversation, while others simply mill about. A voice of recognition calls out from the gloom.

                              THREEPIO
                Artoo-Detoo! It's you! It's you!

A battered Threepio scrambles up to Artoo and embraces him.

EXT. TATOOINE — ROCK CANYON — SANDCRAWLER — SUNSET

The enormous sandcrawler lumbers off toward the magnificent twin
suns, which are slowly setting over a distant mountain ridge.

EXT. TATOOINE — DESERT — DAY   ← Start replacement scene I from
                                                  page 18A for the Special Edition

Four Imperial stormtroopers mill about in front of the half-buried
lifepod that brought Artoo and Threepio to Tatooine. A trooper yells
to an officer some distance away.

                    FIRST TROOPER
          Someone was in the pod. The tracks go off in
          this direction.

A second trooper picks a small bit of metal out of the sand and
gives it to the first trooper.

                    SECOND TROOPER
          Look, sir — droids.
                                                ← End replacement scene
                                                  Special Edition

EXT. TATOOINE — DUNES   ← Replace with insert II
                                                  from page 18A for the
The sandcrawler moves slowly down a great sand dune.   Special Edition

INT. SANDCRAWLER

Threepio and Artoo noisily bounce along inside the cramped prison
chamber. Artoo appears to be shut off.

                    THREEPIO
          Wake up! Wake up!

Suddenly the shaking and bouncing of the sandcrawler stops, creating
quite a commotion among the mechanical men. Threepio's fist bangs
the head of Artoo whose computer lights pop on as he begins beeping.
At the far end of the long chamber a hatch opens, filling the
chamber with blinding white light. A dozen or so Jawas make their
way through the odd assortment of robots.

                    THREEPIO
          We're doomed.

A Jawa starts moving toward them.

                    THREEPIO
          Do you think they'll melt us down?

Artoo responds, making beeping sounds.

                                                          (CONTINUED)

CONTINUED:

>   THREEPIO
>   Don't shoot! Don't shoot! Will this never
>   end?

EXT. TATOOINE — DESERT — LARS HOMESTEAD — AFTERNOON

The Jawas mutter gibberish as they busily line up their battered captives, including Artoo and Threepio, in front of the enormous sandcrawler, which is parked beside a small homestead consisting of three large holes in the ground surrounded by several tall moisture vaporators and one small adobe block house.

The Jawas scurry around fussing over the robots, straightening them up or brushing some dust from a dented metallic elbow. The shrouded little creatures smell horribly, attracting small insects to the dark areas where their mouths and nostrils should be.

Out of the shadows of a dingy side-building limps Owen Lars, a large burly man in his mid-fifties. His reddish eyes are sunken in a dust-covered face. As the farmer carefully inspects each of the robots, he is closely followed by his slump-shouldered nephew, Luke Skywalker. One of the vile little Jawas walks ahead of the farmer spouting an animated sales pitch in a queer, unintelligible language.

A voice calls out from one of the huge holes that form the homestead. Luke goes over to the edge and sees his aunt Beru standing in the main courtyard.

>   BERU
>   Luke, tell Owen that if he gets a translator
>   to be sure it speaks Bocce.

>   LUKE
>   It looks like we don't have much of a choice
>   but I'll remind him.

Luke returns to his uncle as they look over the equipment for sale with the Jawa leader.

>   OWEN
>   I have no need for a protocol droid.

>   THREEPIO
>   (quickly) Sir — not in an environment such
>   as this — that's why I've also been
>   programmed for over thirty secondary
>   functions that . . .

>   OWEN
>   What I really need is a droid that under-
>   stands the binary language of moisture
>   vaporators.

                                                    (CONTINUED)

SPECIAL EDITION INSERT I TO PAGE 17

EXTERIOR TATOOINE — DESERT — DAY

Imperial stormtroopers mill about in front of the half-buried lifepod that brought Artoo
and Threepio to Tatooine, searching for the droids on foot and mounted on dewbacks. An
Imperial heavy shuttle transport lifts off in the background, wings unfolding as it flies
off. A trooper yells to an officer some distance away.

                              FIRST TROOPER
             Someone was in the pod. The tracks go off in this direction.

A second trooper picks a small bit of metal out of the sand and holds it up.

                              SECOND TROOPER
             Look, sir — droids.

SPECIAL EDITION INSERT II TO PAGE 17

EXTERIOR TATOOINE — DUNES

The sandcrawler moves slowly over the rocky terrain.

CONTINUED:

                       THREEPIO

Vaporators! Sir — My first job was program-
ming binary load lifters . . . very similar
to your vaporators. You could say . . .

                       OWEN

Do you speak Bocce?

                       THREEPIO

Of course I can, sir. It's like a second
language for me . . . I'm as fluent in
Bocce . . .

                       OWEN

All right; shut up! (turning to Jawa) I'll
take this one.

                       THREEPIO

Shutting up, sir.

                       OWEN

Luke, take these two over to the garage, will
you? I want you to have both of them cleaned
up before dinner.

                       LUKE

But I was going into Toshi Station to pick up
some power converters . . .

                       OWEN

You can waste time with your friends when
your chores are done. Now come on, get to it!

                       LUKE

All right, come on! And the red one, come on.
Well, come on, Red, let's go.

As the Jawas start to lead the three remaining robots back into the
sandcrawler, Artoo lets out a pathetic little beep and starts after
his old friend Threepio. He is restrained by a slimy Jawa, who zaps
him with a control box.

Owen is negotiating with the head Jawa. Luke and the two robots
start for the garage when a plate pops off the head of the red
astro-droid, throwing parts all over the ground. He adjusts
the astro-droid's head plate and it sparks wildly.

                       LUKE

Uncle Owen . . .

                       OWEN

Yeah?

                       LUKE

This R2 unit has a bad motivator. Look!

(CONTINUED)

CONTINUED:

> OWEN
> (to the head Jawa) Hey, what're you trying to
> push on us?

The Jawa goes into a loud spiel. Meanwhile, Artoo has sneaked out of
line and is moving up and down trying to attract attention. He lets
out with a low whistle. Threepio taps Luke on the shoulder.

> THREEPIO
> (pointing to Artoo) Excuse me, sir, but that
> R2 unit is in prime condition. A real
> bargain.

> LUKE
> Uncle Owen . . .

> OWEN
> Yeah?

> LUKE
> What about that one?

> OWEN
> (to Jawa) What about that blue one? We'll
> take that one.

With a little reluctance the scruffy dwarf trades the damaged astro-
robot for Artoo.

> LUKE
> Yeah, take this away.

> THREEPIO
> Uh, I'm quite sure you'll be very pleased
> with that one, sir. He really is in first-
> class condition. I've worked with him before.
> Here he comes.

Owen pays off the whining Jawa as Luke and the two robots trudge off
toward a grimy homestead entry.

> LUKE
> Okay, let's go.

> THREEPIO
> (to Artoo) Now, don't forget this! Why I
> should stick my neck out for you is quite
> beyond my capacity!

INT. LARS HOMESTEAD — GARAGE AREA — LATE AFTERNOON

The garage is cluttered and worn, but a friendly peaceful atmosphere
permeates the low gray chamber. Threepio lowers himself into a large
tub filled with warm oil. Near the battered landspeeder little Artoo
rests on a large battery with a cord attached to his face.

CONTINUED:

> **THREEPIO**
> Thank the maker! This oil bath is going to
> feel so good. I've got such a bad case of
> dust contamination, I can barely move!

Artoo beeps a muffled reply. Luke seems to be lost in thought as he
runs his hand over the damaged fin of a small two-man skyhopper
spaceship resting in a low hangar off the garage. Finally Luke's
frustrations get the better of him and he slams a wrench across the
workbench.

> **LUKE**
> It just isn't fair. Oh, Biggs is right. I'm
> never gonna get out of here!

> **THREEPIO**
> Is there anything I might do to help?

Luke glances at the battered robot. A bit of his anger drains and a
tiny smile creeps across his face.

> **LUKE**
> Well, not unless you can alter time, speed up
> the harvest, or teleport me off this rock!

> **THREEPIO**
> I don't think so, sir. I'm only a droid and
> not very knowledgeable about such things. Not
> on this planet, anyway. As a matter of fact,
> I'm not even sure which planet I'm on.

> **LUKE**
> Well, if there's a bright center to the
> universe, you're on the planet that it's
> farthest from.

> **THREEPIO**
> I see, sir.

> **LUKE**
> Uh, you can call me Luke.

> **THREEPIO**
> I see, Sir Luke.

> **LUKE**
> (laughing) Just Luke.

> **THREEPIO**
> And I am See-Threepio, human-cyborg
> relations, and this is my counterpart, Artoo-
> Detoo.

> **LUKE**
> Hello.

Artoo beeps in response. Luke unplugs Artoo and begins to scrape
several connectors on the robot's head with a chrome pick. Threepio

(CONTINUED)

CONTINUED:

climbs out of the oil tub and begins wiping oil from his bronze
body.

                    LUKE
          You got a lot of carbon scoring here. It
          looks like you boys have seen a lot of
          action.

                    THREEPIO
          With all we've been through, sometimes I'm
          amazed we're in as good condition as we are,
          what with the Rebellion and all.

Luke sparks to life at the mention of the Rebellion.

                    LUKE
          You know of the Rebellion against the Empire?

                    THREEPIO
          That's how we came to be in your service, if
          you take my meaning, sir.

                    LUKE
          Have you been in many battles?

                    THREEPIO
          Several, I think. Actually, there's not much
          to tell. I'm not much more than an inter-
          preter, and not very good at telling stories.
          Well, not at making them interesting, anyway.

Luke struggles to remove a small metal fragment from Artoo's neck
joint. He uses a larger pick.

                    LUKE
          Well, my little friend, you've got something
          jammed in here real good. Were you on a
          starcruiser or . . .

The fragment breaks loose with a snap, sending Luke tumbling head
over heels. He sits up and sees a twelve-inch three-dimensional
hologram of Leia Organa, the Rebel senator, being projected from the
face of little Artoo. The image is a rainbow of colors as it
flickers and jiggles in the dimly lit garage. Luke's mouth hangs
open in awe.

                    LEIA
          Help me, Obi-Wan Kenobi. You're my only hope.

                    LUKE
          What's this?

Artoo looks around and sheepishly beeps an answer for Threepio to
translate. Leia continues to repeat the sentence fragment over and
over.

(CONTINUED)

CONTINUED:

> THREEPIO
> What is what?!? He asked you a question . . .
> (pointing at Leia) What is that?

Artoo whistles his surprise as he pretends to just notice the
hologram. He looks around and sheepishly beeps an answer for
Threepio to translate. Leia continues to repeat the sentence
fragment over and over.

> LEIA
> Help me, Obi-Wan Kenobi. You're my only hope.
> Help me, Obi-Wan Kenobi. You're my only hope.

> THREEPIO
> Oh, he says it's nothing, sir. Merely a
> malfunction. Old data. Pay it no mind.

Luke becomes intrigued by the beautiful young girl.

> LUKE
> Who is she? She's beautiful.

> THREEPIO
> I'm afraid I'm not quite sure, sir.

> LEIA
> Help me, Obi-Wan Kenobi . . .

> THREEPIO
> I think she was a passenger on our last
> voyage. A person of some importance, sir —
> I believe. Our captain was attached to . . .

> LUKE
> Is there more to this recording?

Luke reaches for Artoo but he lets out several frantic squeaks and a
whistle.

> THREEPIO
> Behave yourself, Artoo. You're going to get
> us in trouble. It's all right, you can trust
> him. He's our new master.

Artoo whistles and beeps a long message to Threepio.

> THREEPIO
> He says he's the property of Obi-Wan Kenobi,
> a resident of these parts. And it's a private
> message for him. Quite frankly, sir, I don't
> know what he's talking about. Our last master
> was Captain Antilles, but with what we've
> been through, this little R2 unit has become
> a bit eccentric.

> LUKE
> Obi-Wan Kenobi? I wonder if he means old Ben
> Kenobi?

(CONTINUED)

CONTINUED:

                        THREEPIO
        I beg your pardon, sir, but do you know what
        he's talking about?

                        LUKE
        Well, I don't know anyone named Obi-Wan, but
        old Ben lives out beyond the Dune Sea. He's
        kind of a strange old hermit.

Luke gazes at the beautiful young princess for a few moments.

                        LUKE
        I wonder who she is. It sounds like she's in
        trouble. I'd better play back the whole
        thing.

Artoo beeps something to Threepio.

                        THREEPIO
        He says the restraining bolt has short
        circuited his recording system. He suggests
        that if you remove the bolt, he might be able
        to play back the entire recording.

Luke looks longingly at the lovely little princess and hasn't really
heard what Threepio has been saying.

                        LUKE
        H'm? Oh, yeah, well, I guess you're too small
        to run away on me if I take this off! Okay.

Luke takes a wedged bar and pops the restraining bolt off Artoo's
side.

                        LUKE
        There you go.

The princess immediately disappears . . .

                        LUKE
        Well, wait a minute. Where'd she go? Bring
        her back! Play back the entire message.

Artoo beeps an innocent reply as Threepio sits up in embarrassment.

                        THREEPIO
        What message? The one you've just been
        playing. The one you're carrying inside your
        rusty innards!

A woman's voice calls out from the other room.

                      AUNT BERU
      Luke? Luke! Come to dinner!

Luke stands up and shakes his head at the malfunctioning robot.

CONTINUED:

                    LUKE
        All right, I'll be right there, Aunt Beru.

                    THREEPIO
        I'm sorry, sir, but he appears to have picked
        up a slight flutter.

Luke tosses Artoo's restraining bolt on the workbench and hurries
out of the room.

                    LUKE
        Well, see what you can do with him. I'll be
        right back.

                    THREEPIO
        (to Artoo) Just you reconsider playing that
        message for him.

Artoo beeps in response.

                    THREEPIO
        No, I don't think he likes you at all.

Artoo beeps.

                    THREEPIO
        No, I don't like you either.

INT. LARS HOMESTEAD — DINING AREA

Luke's aunt Beru, a warm, motherly woman, fills a pitcher with blue
fluid from a refrigerated container in the well-used kitchen. She
puts the pitcher on a tray with some bowls of food and starts for
the dining area.

Luke sits with his uncle Owen before a table covered with steaming
bowls of food as Aunt Beru carries in a bowl of red grain.

                    LUKE
        You know, I think that R2 unit we bought
        might have been stolen.

                    OWEN
        What makes you think that?

                    LUKE
        Well, I stumbled across a recording while I
        was cleaning him. He says he belongs to
        someone called Obi-Wan Kenobi.

Owen is greatly alarmed at the mention of this name, but manages to
control himself.

                    LUKE
        I thought he might have meant old Ben. Do you
        know what he's talking about? Well, I wonder
        if he's related to Ben.

                                              (CONTINUED)

CONTINUED:

Owen breaks loose with a fit of uncontrolled anger.

> OWEN
> That old man's just a crazy wizard. Tomorrow
> I want you to take that R2 unit into Anchor-
> head and have its memory flushed. That'll be
> the end of it. It belongs to us now.

> LUKE
> But what if this Obi-Wan comes looking for
> him?

> OWEN
> He won't. I don't think he exists anymore. He
> died about the same time as your father.

> LUKE
> He knew my father?

> OWEN
> I told you to forget it. Your only concern is
> to prepare the new droids for tomorrow. In
> the morning I want them on the south ridge
> working on those condensers.

> LUKE
> Yes, sir. I think those new droids are going
> to work out fine. In fact, I, uh, was also
> thinking about our agreement about my staying
> on another season. And if these new droids do
> work out, I want to transmit my application
> to the Academy this year.

Owen's face becomes a scowl, although he tries to suppress it.

> OWEN
> You mean the next semester before harvest?

> LUKE
> Sure, there're more than enough droids.

> OWEN
> Harvest is when I need you the most. Only one
> more season. This year we'll make enough on
> the harvest so I'll be able to hire some more
> hands. And then you can go to the Academy
> next year.

Luke continues to toy with his food, not looking at his uncle.

> OWEN
> You must understand I need you here, Luke.

> LUKE
> But it's a whole 'nother year.

> OWEN
> Look, it's only one more season.

(CONTINUED)

CONTINUED:

Luke pushes his half-eaten plate of food aside and stands.

                    LUKE
          Yeah, that's what you said last year when
          Biggs and Tank left.

                    AUNT BERU
          Where are you going?

                    LUKE
          It looks like I'm going nowhere. I have to
          finish cleaning those droids.

Resigned to his fate, Luke paddles out of the room. Owen mechani-
cally finishes his dinner.

                    AUNT BERU
          Owen, he can't stay here forever. Most of his
          friends have gone. It means so much to him.

                    OWEN
          I'll make it up to him next year. I promise.

                    AUNT BERU
          Luke's just not a farmer, Owen. He has too
          much of his father in him.

                    OWEN
          That's what I'm afraid of.

EXT. TATOOINE — LARS HOMESTEAD

The giant twin suns of Tatooine slowly disappear behind a distant
dune range. Luke stands watching them for a few moments, then reluc-
tantly enters the domed entrance to the homestead.

INT. LARS HOMESTEAD — GARAGE

Luke enters the garage to discover the robots nowhere in sight. He
takes a small control box from his utility belt similar to the one
the Jawas were carrying. He activates the box, which creates a low
hum, and Threepio, letting out a short yell, pops up from behind the
skyhopper spaceship.

                    LUKE
          What are you doing hiding there?

Threepio stumbles forward, but Artoo is still nowhere in sight.

                    THREEPIO
          It wasn't my fault, sir. Please don't deacti-
          vate me. I told him not to go, but he's
                    (MORE)

                                                    (CONTINUED)

CONTINUED:

> THREEPIO (CONT'D)
> faulty, malfunctioning; kept babbling on
> about his mission.

> LUKE

> Oh, no!

Luke races out of the garage followed by Threepio.

EXT. TATOOINE — LARS HOMESTEAD

Luke rushes out of the small domed entry to the homestead and
searches the darkening horizon for the small triped astro-robot.
Threepio struggles out of the homestead and on the salt flat as Luke
scans the landscape with his electrobinoculars.

> THREEPIO
> That R2 unit has always been a problem. These
> astro-droids are getting quite out of hand.
> Even I can't understand their logic at times.

> LUKE
> How could I be so stupid? He's nowhere in
> sight. Blast it!

> THREEPIO
> Pardon me, sir, but couldn't we go after him?

> LUKE
> It's too dangerous with all the Sand People
> around. We'll have to wait until morning.

Owen yells up from the homestead plaza.

> OWEN
> Luke, I'm shutting the power down for the
> night.

> LUKE
> All right, I'll be there in a few minutes.
> Boy, am I gonna get it.

He takes one final look across the dim horizon.

> LUKE
> You know that little droid is going to cause
> me a lot of trouble.

> THREEPIO
> Oh, he excels at that, sir.

INT. LARS HOMESTEAD — PLAZA

Morning slowly creeps into the sparse but sparkling oasis of the open courtyard. The idyll is broken by the yelling of Uncle Owen, his voice echoing throughout the homestead.

                    OWEN
          Luke? Luke? Luke? Where could he be loafing
          now!

INT. LARS HOMESTEAD — KITCHEN

The interior of the kitchen is a warm glow as Aunt Beru prepares the morning breakfast. Owen enters in a huff.

                    OWEN
          Have you seen Luke this morning?

                    AUNT BERU
          He said he had some things to do before he
          started today, so he left early.

                    OWEN
          Uh? Did he take those two new droids with
          him?

                    AUNT BERU
          I think so.

                    OWEN
          Well, he'd better have those units in the
          south range repaired by midday or there'll be
          hell to pay!

EXT. TATOOINE — DESERT WASTELAND — LUKE'S SPEEDER — DAY

The rock and sand of the desert floor are a blur as Threepio pilots the sleek landspeeder gracefully across the vast wasteland.

INT./EXT. LUKE'S SPEEDER — DESERT WASTELAND — TRAVELING — DAY

Luke leans over the back of the speeder and adjusts something in the motor compartment.

                    LUKE
          (yelling) How's that?

Threepio signals that it is fine and Luke turns back into the wind-whipped cockpit and pops the canopy shut.

(CONTINUED)

CONTINUED:

                              LUKE
          Old Ben Kenobi lives out in this direction
          somewhere, but I don't see how that R2 unit
          could have come this far. We must have missed
          him. Uncle Owen isn't going to take this very
          well.

                            THREEPIO
          Sir, would it help if you told him it was my
          fault?

                              LUKE
          (brightening) Sure. He needs you. He'd
          probably only deactivate you for a day or
          so . . .

                            THREEPIO
          Deactivate! Well, on the other hand, if you
          hadn't removed his restraining bolt . . .

                              LUKE
          Wait, there's something dead ahead on the
          scanner. It looks like our droid . . . hit
          the accelerator.

EXT. TATOOINE — ROCK MESA — DUNE SEA — COASTLINE — DAY

From high on a rock mesa, the tiny landspeeder can be seen gliding
across the desert floor. Suddenly in the foreground two weather-
beaten Sand People shrouded in their grimy desert cloaks peer over
the edge of the rock mesa. One of the marginally human creatures
raises a long ominous laser rifle and points it at the speeder but
the second creature grabs the gun before it can be fired.

The Sand People, or Tusken Raiders as they're sometimes called,
speak in a coarse barbaric language as they get into an animated
argument. The second Tusken Raider seems to get in the final word
and the nomads scurry over the rocky terrain.

EXT. TATOOINE — ROCK MESA — CANYON

The Tusken Raiders approach two large banthas standing tied to a
rock. The monstrous, bear-like creatures are as large as elephants,
with huge red eyes, tremendous looped horns, and long, furry,
dinosaur-like tails. The Tusken Raiders mount saddles strapped to
the huge creatures' shaggy backs and ride off down the rugged bluff.

EXT. TATOOINE — ROCK CANYON — FLOOR

The speeder is parked on the floor of a massive canyon. Luke, with his long laser rifle slung over his shoulder, stands before little Artoo.

                    LUKE
          Hey, whoa, just where do you think you're
          going?

The little droid whistles a feeble reply, as Threepio poses menacingly behind the little runaway.

                    THREEPIO
          Master Luke here is your rightful owner.
          We'll have no more of this Obi-Wan Kenobi
          gibberish . . . and don't talk to me of your
          mission, either. You're fortunate he doesn't
          blast you into a million pieces right here.

                    LUKE
          Well, come on. It's getting late. I only hope
          we can get back before Uncle Owen really
          blows up.

                    THREEPIO
          If you don't mind my saying so, sir, I think
          you should deactivate the little fugitive
          until you've gotten him back to your
          workshop.

                    LUKE
          No, he's not going to try anything.

Suddenly the little robot jumps to life with a mass of frantic whistles and screams.

                    LUKE
          What's wrong with him now?

                    THREEPIO
          Oh my . . . sir, he says there are several
          creatures approaching from the southeast.

Luke swings his rifle into position and looks to the south.

                    LUKE
          Sand People! Or worse! Come on, let's go have
          a look. Come on.

EXT. TATOOINE — ROCK CANYON — RIDGE — DAY

Luke carefully makes his way to the top of a rock ridge and scans

(CONTINUED)

CONTINUED:

the canyon with his electrobinoculars. He spots the two riderless banthas. Threepio struggles up behind the young adventurer.

> LUKE
> There are two banthas down there but I don't
> see any . . . wait a second, they're Sand
> People all right. I can see one of them now.

Luke watches the distant Tusken Raider through his electrobinoculars. Suddenly something huge moves in front of his field of view. Before Luke or Threepio can react, a large, gruesome Tusken Raider looms over them. Threepio is startled and backs away, right off the side of the cliff. He can be heard for several moments as he clangs, bangs and rattles down the side of the mountain.

The towering creature brings down his curved, double-pointed gaderffii — the dreaded axe blade that has struck terror in the heart of the local settlers. But Luke manages to block the blow with his laser rifle, which is smashed to pieces. The terrified farm boy scrambles backward until he is forced to the edge of a deep crevice. The sinister Raider stands over him with his weapon raised and lets out a horrible shrieking laugh.

EXT. TATOOINE — ROCK CANYON — FLOOR — DAY

Artoo forces himself into the shadows of a small alcove in the rocks as the vicious Sand People walk past carrying the inert Luke Skywalker, who is dropped in a heap before the speeder. The Sand People ransack the speeder, throwing parts and supplies in all directions. Suddenly they stop. Then everything is quiet for a few moments. A great howling moan is heard echoing throughout the canyon which sends the Sand People fleeing in terror.

Artoo moves even tighter into the shadows as the slight swishing sound that frightened off the Sand People grows even closer, until a shabby old desert-rat-of-a-man appears and leans over Luke. His ancient leathery face, cracked and weathered by exotic climates, is set off by dark, penetrating eyes and a scraggly white beard. Ben Kenobi squints his eyes as he scrutinizes the unconscious farm boy. Artoo makes a slight sound and Ben turns and looks right at him.

> BEN
> Hello there! Come here, my little friend.
> Don't be afraid.

Artoo waddles over to where Luke lies crumpled in a heap and begins to whistle and beep his concern. Ben puts his hand on Luke's forehead and he begins to come around.

> BEN
> Don't worry, he'll be all right.

(CONTINUED)

CONTINUED:

                    LUKE
What happened?

                    BEN
Rest easy, son, you've had a busy day. You're
fortunate you're still in one piece.

                    LUKE
Ben? Ben Kenobi! Boy, am I glad to see you!

                    BEN
The Jundland Wastes are not to be traveled
lightly. Tell me, young Luke, what brings you
out this far?

                    LUKE
Oh, this little droid! I think he's searching
for his former master . . . I've never seen
such devotion in a droid before . . . there
seems to be no stopping him. He claims to be
the property of an Obi-Wan Kenobi. Is he a
relative of yours? Do you know who he's
talking about?

Ben ponders this for a moment, scratching his scruffy beard.

                    BEN
Obi-Wan Kenobi . . . Obi-Wan? Now that's a
name I haven't heard in a long time . . . a
long time.

                    LUKE
I think my uncle knew him. He said he was
dead . . .

                    BEN
Oh, he's not dead, not . . . not yet.

                    LUKE
You know him!

                    BEN
Well of course, of course I know him. He's
me! I haven't gone by the name Obi-Wan since,
oh, before you were born.

                    LUKE
Then this droid does belong to you.

                    BEN
Don't seem to remember ever owning a droid.
Very interesting . . .

He suddenly looks up at the overhanging cliffs.

(CONTINUED)

CONTINUED:

> BEN
> I think we better get indoors. The Sand
> People are easily startled but they will soon
> be back and in greater numbers.

Luke sits up and rubs his head. Artoo lets out a pathetic beep
causing Luke to remember something. He looks around.

> LUKE
> . . . Threepio!

EXT. TATOOINE — SAND PIT — ROCK MESA — DAY

Little Artoo stands at the edge of a large sand pit and begins to
chatter away in electronic whistles and beeps. Luke and Ben stand
over a very dented and tangled Threepio lying half buried in the
sand. One of his arms has broken off.

Luke tries to revive the inert robot by shaking him and then flips a
hidden switch on his back several times until finally the mechanical
man's systems turn on.

> THREEPIO
> Where am I? I must have taken a bad
> step . . .

> LUKE
> Can you stand? We've got to get out of here
> before the Sand People return.

> THREEPIO
> I don't think I can make it. You go on,
> Master Luke. There's no sense in you risking
> yourself on my account. I'm done for.

Artoo makes a beeping sound.

> LUKE
> No, you're not. What kind of talk is that?

Luke and Ben help the battered robot to his feet. Little Artoo
watches from the top of the pit. Ben glances around suspiciously.
Sensing something, he stands up and sniffs the air.

> BEN
> Quickly, son . . . they're on the move.

INT. KENOBI'S DWELLING

The small, spartan hovel is cluttered with desert junk but still
manages to radiate an air of time-worn comfort and security. Luke is
in one corner repairing Threepio's arm, as old Ben sits thinking.

(CONTINUED)

CONTINUED:

> LUKE
>
> No, my father didn't fight in the wars. He
> was a navigator on a spice freighter.
>
> BEN
>
> That's what your uncle told you. He didn't
> hold with your father's ideals. Thought he
> should have stayed here and not gotten
> involved.
>
> LUKE
>
> You fought in the Clone Wars?
>
> BEN
>
> Yes, I was once a Jedi Knight the same as
> your father.
>
> LUKE
>
> I wish I'd known him.
>
> BEN
>
> He was the best starpilot in the galaxy, and
> a cunning warrior. I understand you've become
> quite a good pilot yourself. And he was a
> good friend. Which reminds me . . .

Ben gets up and goes to a chest where he rummages around. As Luke
finishes repairing Threepio and starts to fit the restraining bolt
back on, Threepio looks at him nervously. Luke thinks about the bolt
for a moment then puts it on the table. Ben shuffles up and presents
Luke with a short handle with several electronic gadgets attached
to it.

> BEN
>
> I have something here for you. Your father
> wanted you to have this when you were old
> enough, but your uncle wouldn't allow it. He
> feared you might follow old Obi-Wan on some
> damned-fool idealistic crusade like your
> father did.
>
> THREEPIO
>
> Sir, if you'll not be needing me, I'll close
> down for a while.
>
> LUKE
>
> Sure, go ahead.

Ben hands Luke the saber.

> LUKE
>
> What is it?
>
> BEN
>
> Your father's lightsaber. This is the weapon
> (MORE)

(CONTINUED)

CONTINUED:

                    BEN (CONT'D)
          of a Jedi Knight. Not as clumsy or as random
          as a blaster.

Luke pushes a button on the handle. A long beam shoots out about
four feet and flickers there. The light plays across the ceiling.

                    BEN
          An elegant weapon for a more civilized time.
          For over a thousand generations the Jedi
          Knights were the guardians of peace and
          justice in the Old Republic. Before the dark
          times, before the Empire.

Luke hasn't really been listening.

                    LUKE
          How did my father die?

                    BEN
          A young Jedi named Darth Vader, who was a
          pupil of mine until he turned to evil, helped
          the Empire hunt down and destroy the Jedi
          Knights. He betrayed and murdered your
          father. Now the Jedi are all but extinct.
          Vader was seduced by the dark side of the
          Force.

                    LUKE
          The Force?

                    BEN
          Well, the Force is what gives the Jedi his
          power. It's an energy field created by all
          living things. It surrounds us and penetrates
          us. It binds the galaxy together.

Artoo makes beeping sounds.

                    BEN
          Now, let's see if we can't figure out what
          you are, my little friend. And where you come
          from.

                    LUKE
          I saw part of the message he was . . .

Luke is cut short as the recorded image of the beautiful young Rebel
princess is projected from Artoo's face.

                    BEN
          I seem to have found it.

Luke stops his work as the lovely girl's image flickers before his
eyes.

(CONTINUED)

CONTINUED:

                         LEIA
          General Kenobi, years ago you served my
          father in the Clone Wars. Now he begs you to
          help him in his struggle against the Empire.
          I regret that I am unable to present my
          father's request to you in person, but my
          ship has fallen under attack and I'm afraid
          my mission to bring you to Alderaan has
          failed. I have placed information vital to
          the survival of the Rebellion into the memory
          systems of this R2 unit. My father will know
          how to retrieve it. You must see this droid
          safely delivered to him on Alderaan. This is
          our most desperate hour. Help me, Obi-Wan
          Kenobi. You're my only hope.

There is a little static and the transmission is cut short. Old Ben
leans back and scratches his head. He silently puffs on a tarnished
chrome water pipe. Luke has stars in his eyes.

                         BEN
          You must learn the ways of the Force if
          you're to come with me to Alderaan.

                         LUKE
          (laughing) Alderaan? I'm not going to
          Alderaan. I've got to go home. It's late, I'm
          in for it as it is.

                         BEN
          I need your help, Luke. She needs your help.
          I'm getting too old for this sort of thing.

                         LUKE
          I can't get involved! I've got work to do!
          It's not that I like the Empire. I hate it!
          But there's nothing I can do about it right
          now. It's such a long way from here.

                         BEN
          That's your uncle talking.

                         LUKE
          (sighing) Oh, God, my uncle. How am I ever
          going to explain this?

                         BEN
          Learn about the Force, Luke.

                         LUKE
          Look, I can take you as far as Anchorhead.
          You can get a transport there to Mos Eisley
          or wherever you're going.

CONTINUED:

                              BEN
          You must do what you feel is right, of
          course.

EXT. SPACE

An Imperial Star Destroyer heads toward the evil planet-like battle
station: the Death Star!

INT. DEATH STAR — CONFERENCE ROOM

Eight Imperial senators and generals sit around a black conference
table. Imperial stormtroopers stand guard around the room. Commander
Tagge, a young, slimy-looking general, is speaking.

                           TAGGE
          Until this battle station is fully opera-
          tional we are vulnerable. The Rebel Alliance
          is too well equipped. They're more dangerous
          than you realize.

The bitter Admiral Motti twists nervously in his chair.

                           MOTTI
          Dangerous to your starfleet, Commander; not
          to this battle station!

                           TAGGE
          The Rebellion will continue to gain support
          in the Imperial Senate as long as . . .

Suddenly all heads turn as Commander Tagge's speech is cut short and
the Grand Moff Tarkin, governor of the Imperial outland regions,
enters. He is followed by his powerful ally, the Sith Lord, Darth
Vader. All of the generals stand and bow before the thin, evil-
looking governor as he takes his place at the head of the table. The
Dark Lord stands behind him.

                         TARKIN
          The Imperial Senate will no longer be of any
          concern to us. I've just received word that
          the Emperor has dissolved the council perma-
          nently. The last remnants of the Old Republic
          have been swept away.

                           TAGGE
          That's impossible! How will the Emperor
          maintain control without the bureaucracy?

                         TARKIN
          The regional governors now have direct
          control over territories. Fear will keep the
                    (MORE)

(CONTINUED)

CONTINUED:

                    TARKIN (CONT'D)
local systems in line. Fear of this battle
station.

                    TAGGE
And what of the Rebellion? If the Rebels have
obtained a complete technical readout of this
station, it is possible, however unlikely,
that they might find a weakness and exploit
it.

                    VADER
The plans you refer to will soon be back in
our hands.

                    MOTTI
Any attack made by the Rebels against this
station would be a useless gesture, no matter
what technical data they've obtained. This
station is now the ultimate power in the
universe. I suggest we use it!

                    VADER
Don't be too proud of this technological
terror you've constructed. The ability to
destroy a planet is insignificant next to the
power of the Force.

                    MOTTI
Don't try to frighten us with your sorcerer's
ways, Lord Vader. Your sad devotion to that
ancient religion has not helped you conjure
up the stolen data tapes, or given you clair-
voyance enough to find the Rebels' hidden
fort . . .

Suddenly Motti chokes and starts to turn blue under Vader's spell.

                    VADER
I find your lack of faith disturbing.

                    TARKIN
Enough of this! Vader, release him!

                    VADER
As you wish.

                    TARKIN
This bickering is pointless. Lord Vader will
provide us with the location of the Rebel
fortress by the time this station is operational. We will then crush the Rebellion with
one swift stroke.

EXT. TATOOINE — WASTELAND

The speeder stops before what remains of the huge Jawa sandcrawler.
Luke and Ben walk among the smoldering rubble and scattered bodies.

                    LUKE
          It looks like Sand People did this, all
          right. Look, here are gaffi sticks, bantha
          tracks. It's just . . . I never heard of them
          hitting anything this big before.

Ben is crouching in the sand studying the tracks.

                    BEN
          They didn't. But we are meant to think they
          did. These tracks are side by side. Sand
          People always ride single file to hide their
          numbers.

                    LUKE
          These are the same Jawas that sold us Artoo
          and Threepio.

                    BEN
          And these blast points, too accurate for Sand
          People. Only Imperial stormtroopers are so
          precise.

                    LUKE
          Why would Imperial troops want to slaughter
          Jawas?

Luke looks back at the speeder where Artoo and Threepio are inspect-
ing the dead Jawas, and puts two and two together.

                    LUKE
          If they traced the robots here, they may have
          learned who they sold them to. And that would
          lead them back home!

Luke reaches a sudden horrible realization, then races for the
speeder and jumps in.

                    BEN
          Wait, Luke! It's too dangerous.

Luke races off leaving Ben and the two robots alone with the burning
sandcrawler.

EXT. TATOOINE — WASTELAND

Luke races across the flat landscape in his battered landspeeder.

EXT. TATOOINE — LARS HOMESTEAD

The speeder roars up to the burning homestead. Luke jumps out and
runs to the smoking holes that were once his home. Debris is
scattered everywhere and it looks as if a great battle has taken
place.

                         LUKE
          Uncle Owen! Aunt Beru! Uncle Owen!

Luke stumbles around in a daze looking for his aunt and uncle.
Suddenly he comes upon their smoldering remains. He is stunned, and
cannot speak. Hate replaces fear and a new resolve comes over him.

EXT. SPACE

Imperial TIE fighters race toward the Death Star.

INT. DEATH STAR — DETENTION CORRIDOR

Two stormtroopers open an electronic cell door and allow several
Imperial guards to enter. Princess Leia's face is filled with
defiance, which slowly gives way to fear as a giant black torture
robot enters, followed by Darth Vader.

                         VADER
          And now, Your Highness, we will discuss the
          location of your hidden Rebel base.

The torture robot gives off a steady beeping sound as it approaches
Princess Leia and extends one of its mechanical arms bearing a large
hypodermic needle. The door slides shut and the long cell block
hallway appears peaceful. The muffled screams of the Rebel princess
are barely heard.

EXT. TATOOINE — WASTELAND

There is a large bonfire of Jawa bodies blazing in front of the
sandcrawler as Ben and the robots finish burning the dead. Luke
drives up in the speeder and Ben walks over to him.

                         BEN
          There's nothing you could have done, Luke,
          had you been there. You'd have been killed,
          too, and the droids would now be in the hands
          of the Empire.

                         LUKE
          I want to come with you to Alderaan. There's
          nothing here for me now. I want to learn the
                         (MORE)

                                              (CONTINUED)

CONTINUED:

                    LUKE (CONT'D)
          ways of the Force and become a Jedi like my
          father.

EXT. TATOOINE — WASTELAND

The landspeeder with Luke, Artoo, Threepio, and Ben in it zooms
across the desert. The speeder stops on a bluff overlooking the
spaceport at Mos Eisley. It is a haphazard array of low, gray,
concrete structures and semi-domes. A harsh gale blows across the
stark canyon floor. Luke adjusts his goggles and walks to the edge
of the craggy bluff where Ben is standing.

                    BEN
          Mos Eisley Spaceport. You will never find a
          more wretched hive of scum and villainy. We
          must be cautious.

Ben looks over at Luke, who gives the old Jedi a determined smile.

                                    ← Insert I from page 42A for the Special Edition
EXT. TATOOINE — MOS EISLEY — STREET
                                    ← Insert II from page 42A for the Special Edition
The speeder is stopped on a crowded street by several combat-
hardened stormtroopers who look over the two robots. A trooper
questions Luke.

                    TROOPER
          How long have you had these droids?

                    LUKE
          About three or four seasons.

                    BEN
          They're for sale if you want them.

                    TROOPER
          Let me see your identification.

Luke becomes very nervous as he fumbles to find his ID while Ben
speaks to the trooper in a very controlled voice.

                    BEN
          You don't need to see his identification.

                    TROOPER
          We don't need to see his identification.

                    BEN
          These are not the droids you're looking for.

                    TROOPER
          These are not the droids we're looking for.

                    BEN
          He can go about his business.

                                              (CONTINUED)

SPECIAL EDITION INSERT I TO PAGE 42

EXT. TATOOINE — MOS EISLEY — APPROACH TO SPACEPORT

The landspeeder zooms into the spaceport of Mos Eisley, scattering small scurriers, that jump to get out of the way.

EXT. TATOOINE — MOS EISLEY — MAIN STREET

The landspeeder heads toward the cantina, passing domed structures, circular landing bays, and an asp droid that gets into an argument with a passing probe droid.

EXT. TATOOINE — MOS EISLEY — STREET

Two Jawas ride a large ronto, an unusual beast of burden, that rears up as a speeder bike veers in front of it, tossing one Jawa off its back onto the ground as the second Jawa swings forward under the ronto's head, holding on to the reins.

SPECIAL EDITION INSERT II TO PAGE 42

Luke pilots his landspeeder carrying Ben and the two droids into the center of the spaceport, past a large crashed vehicle, winding his way among various rontos taking up much of the street. A starship, the Outrider, takes off overhead.

CONTINUED:

                    TROOPER
         You can go about your business.

                    BEN
         (to Luke) Move along.

                    TROOPER
         Move along. Move along.

EXT. TATOOINE — MOS EISLEY — STREET

The speeder pulls up in front of a rundown blockhouse cantina on the
outskirts of the spaceport. Various strange forms of transport,
including several unusual beasts of burden, are parked outside the
bar. A Jawa runs up and begins to fondle the speeder.

                    THREEPIO
         I can't abide these Jawas. Disgusting
         creatures.

As Luke gets out of the speeder he tries to shoo the Jawa away.

                    LUKE
         Go on, go on. I can't understand how we got
         by those troopers. I thought we were dead.

                    BEN
         The Force can have a strong influence on the
         weak-minded. You will find it a powerful
         ally.

                    LUKE
         Do you really think we're going to find a
         pilot here that'll take us to Alderaan?

                    BEN
         Well, most of the best freighter pilots can
         be found here. Only watch your step. This
         place can be a little rough.

                    LUKE
         I'm ready for anything.

                    THREEPIO
         Come along, Artoo.

INT. TATOOINE — MOS EISLEY — CANTINA

The young adventurer and his two mechanical servants follow Ben
Kenobi into the smoke-filled cantina. The murky, moldy den is filled
with a startling array of weird and exotic alien creatures and
monsters at the long metallic bar. At first the sight is horrifying.
One-eyed, thousand-eyed, slimy, furry, scaly, tentacled, and clawed

                                                        (CONTINUED)

CONTINUED:

creatures huddle over drinks. Ben moves to an empty spot at the bar
near a group of repulsive but human scum. A huge, rough-looking
bartender stops Luke and the robots.

                    BARTENDER
        We don't serve their kind here!

Luke, still recovering from the shock of seeing so many outlandish
creatures, doesn't quite catch the bartender's drift.

                    LUKE
        What?

                    BARTENDER
        Your droids. They'll have to wait outside. We
        don't want them here.

Luke looks to old Ben, who is busy talking to one of the Galactic
pirates. He notices that several of the gruesome creatures along the
bar are giving him a very unfriendly glare.

Luke pats Threepio on the shoulder.

                    LUKE
        Listen, why don't you wait out by the
        speeder. We don't want any trouble.

                    THREEPIO
        I heartily agree with you sir.

Threepio and his stubby partner go outside and most of the creatures
at the bar go back to their drinks.

Ben is standing next to Chewbacca, an eight-foot-tall savage-looking
creature resembling a huge gray bushbaby monkey with fierce baboon-
like fangs. His large blue eyes dominate a fur-covered face and
soften his otherwise awesome appearance. Over his matted, furry body
he wears two chrome bandoliers, and little else. He is a 200-year-
old Wookiee and a sight to behold.

Ben speaks to the Wookiee, pointing to Luke several times during his
conversation and the huge creature suddenly lets out a horrifying
laugh. Luke is more than a little bit disconcerted and pretends not
to hear the conversation between Ben and the giant Wookiee.

Luke is terrified but tries not to show it. He quietly sips his
drink, looking over the crowd for a more sympathetic ear or
whatever.

A large, multiple-eyed creature gives Luke a rough shove.

                    CREATURE
        Negola dewaghi wooldugger?!?

The hideous freak is obviously drunk. Luke tries to ignore the
creature and turns back to his drink. A short, grubby human and an
even smaller rodent-like beast join the belligerent monstrosity.

                                            (CONTINUED)

CONTINUED:

> HUMAN
> He doesn't like you.

> LUKE
> I'm sorry.

> HUMAN
> I don't like you either.

The big creature is getting agitated and yells some unintelligible gibberish at the now rather nervous, young adventurer.

> HUMAN
> (continued) Don't insult us. You just watch
> yourself. We're wanted men. I have the death
> sentence on twelve systems.

> LUKE
> I'll be careful then.

> HUMAN
> You'll be dead.

The rodent lets out a loud grunt and everything at the bar moves away. Luke tries to remain cool but it isn't easy. His three adversaries ready their weapons. Old Ben moves in behind Luke.

> BEN
> This little one isn't worth the effort. Come
> let me buy you something . . .

A powerful blow from the unpleasant creature sends the young would-be Jedi sailing across the room, crashing through tables and breaking a large jug filled with a foul-looking liquid. With a blood-curdling shriek, the monster draws a wicked chrome laser pistol from his belt and levels it at old Ben. The bartender panics.

> BARTENDER
> No blasters! No blasters!

With astounding agility old Ben's laser sword sparks to life and in a flash an arm lies on the floor. The rodent is cut in two and the giant multiple-eyed creature lies doubled, cut from chin to groin. Ben carefully and precisely turns off his laser sword and replaces it on his utility belt. Luke, shaking and totally amazed at the old man's abilities, attempts to stand. The entire fight has lasted only a matter of seconds. The cantina goes back to normal, although Ben is given a respectable amount of room at the bar. Luke, rubbing his bruised head, approaches the old man with new awe. Ben points to the Wookiee.

> BEN
> This is Chewbacca. He's first-mate on a ship
> that might suit our needs.

EXT. TATOOINE — MOS EISLEY — STREET

Threepio paces in front of the cantina as Artoo carries on an electronic conversation with another little red astro-droid. A creature comes out of the cantina and approaches two stormtroopers in the street.

                    THREEPIO
          I don't like the look of this.

INT. TATOOINE — MOS EISLEY — CANTINA

Strange creatures play exotic big band music on odd-looking instruments as Luke, still giddy, downs a fresh drink and follows Ben and Chewbacca to a booth where Han Solo is sitting. Han is a tough, roguish starpilot about thirty years old. A mercenary on a starship, he is simple, sentimental, and cocksure.

                    HAN
          Han Solo. I'm captain of the Millennium
          Falcon. Chewie here tells me you're looking
          for passage to the Alderaan system.

                    BEN
          Yes, indeed. If it's a fast ship.

                    HAN
          Fast ship? You've never heard of the Millen-
          nium Falcon?

                    BEN
          Should I have?

                    HAN
          It's the ship that made the Kessel run in
          less than twelve parsecs!

Ben reacts to Solo's stupid attempt to impress them with obvious misinformation.

                    HAN
          (continued) I've outrun Imperial starships,
          not the local bulk-cruisers, mind you. I'm
          talking about the big Corellian ships now.
          She's fast enough for you, old man. What's
          the cargo?

                    BEN
          Only passengers. Myself, the boy, two droids,
          and no questions asked.

                    HAN
          What is it? Some kind of local trouble?

                                        (CONTINUED)

                    BEN
Let's just say we'd like to avoid any
Imperial entanglements.

                    HAN
Well, that's the real trick, isn't it? And
it's going to cost you something extra. Ten
thousand in advance.

                    LUKE
Ten thousand? We could almost buy our own
ship for that!

                    HAN
But who's going to fly it, kid! You?

                    LUKE
You bet I could. I'm not such a bad pilot
myself! We don't have to sit here and
listen . . .

                    BEN
We haven't that much with us. But we could
pay you two thousand now, plus fifteen when
we reach Alderaan.

                    HAN
Seventeen, huh!

Han ponders this for a few moments.

                    HAN
Okay. You guys got yourself a ship. We'll
leave as soon as you're ready. Docking Bay
Ninety-four.

                    BEN
Ninety-four.

                    HAN
Looks like somebody's beginning to take an
interest in your handiwork.

Ben and Luke turn around to see four Imperial stormtroopers looking
at the dead bodies and asking the bartenders some questions. The
bartender points to the booth.

                    TROOPER
All right, we'll check it out.

The stormtroopers look over at the booth but Luke and Ben are gone.
The bartender shrugs his shoulders in puzzlement.

                    HAN
Seventeen thousand! Those guys must really be
desperate. This could really save my neck.
Get back to the ship and get her ready.

EXT. TATOOINE — MOS EISLEY — STREET

                         BEN
        You'll have to sell your speeder.

                         LUKE
        That's okay. I'm never coming back to this
        planet again.

INT. MOS EISLEY — CANTINA

As Han is about to leave, Greedo, a slimy green-faced alien with a
short trunk-nose, pokes a gun in his side. The creature speaks in a
foreign tongue translated into English subtitles.

                       GREEDO
        Going somewhere, Solo?

                       HAN
        Yes, Greedo. As a matter of fact, I was just
        going to see your boss. Tell Jabba that I've
        got his money.

Han sits down and the alien sits across from him holding the gun
on him.

                       GREEDO
        It's too late. You should have paid him when
        you had the chance. Jabba's put a price on
        your head, so large that every bounty hunter
        in the galaxy will be looking for you. I'm
        lucky I found you first.

                       HAN
        Yeah, but this time I got the money.

                       GREEDO
        If you give it to me, I might forget I found
        you.

                       HAN
        I don't have it with me. Tell Jabba . . .

                       GREEDO
        Jabba's through with you. He has no time for
        smugglers who drop their shipments at the
        first sign of an Imperial cruiser.

                       HAN
        Even I get boarded sometimes. Do you think I
        had a choice?

Han Solo slowly reaches for his gun under the table.

(CONTINUED)

CONTINUED:

                    GREEDO
          You can tell that to Jabba. He may only take
          your ship.

                    HAN
          Over my dead body.

                    GREEDO
          That's the idea. I've been looking forward to
          killing you for a long time.

                    HAN
          Yes, I'll bet you have.

Suddenly the slimy alien disappears in a blinding flash of light. ← Replace with
Han pulls his smoking gun from beneath the table as the other   insert from
patrons look on in bemused amazement. Han gets up and starts   page 50A for
out of the cantina, flipping the bartender some coins as he   Special Edition.
leaves.

                    HAN
          Sorry about the mess.

EXT. SPACE

Several TIE fighters approach the Death Star.

INT. DEATH STAR — CONTROL ROOM

                    VADER
          Her resistance to the mind probe is consider-
          able. It will be some time before we can
          extract any information from her.

An Imperial Officer interrupts the meeting.

                    IMPERIAL OFFICER
          The final check-out is completed. All systems
          are operational. What course shall we set?

                    TARKIN
          Perhaps she would respond to an alternative
          form of persuasion.

                    VADER
          What do you mean?

                    TARKIN
          I think it is time we demonstrated the full
          power of this station. (to soldier) Set your
          course for Princess Leia's home planet of
          Alderaan.

(CONTINUED)

CONTINUED:

                    TROOPER
        With pleasure.

EXT. TATOOINE — MOS EISLEY — STREET

Four heavily-armed stormtroopers move menacingly along a narrow slum
alleyway crowded with darkly clad creatures hawking exotic goods in
dingy little stalls. Men, monsters, and robots crouch in waste-
filled doorways, whispering and hiding from the hot winds.

                    THREEPIO
        Lock the door, Artoo.

One of the troopers checks a tightly locked door and moves on down
the alleyway. The door slides open a crack and Threepio peeks out.
Artoo is barely visible in the background.

                    TROOPER
        All right, check that side of the street.
        It's secure. Move on to the next one.

The door opens; Threepio moves into the doorway.

                    THREEPIO
        I would much rather have gone with Master
        Luke than stay here with you. I don't know
        what all this trouble is about, but I'm sure
        it must be your fault.

Artoo makes beeping sounds.

                    THREEPIO
        You watch your language!

EXT. TATOOINE — MOS EISLEY — STREET — ALLEYWAY — USED SPEEDER LOT

Ben and Luke are standing in a sleazy used speeder lot, talking with
a tall, grotesque, insect-like used speeder dealer. Strange exotic
bodies and spindly-legged beasts pass by as the insect concludes the
sale by giving Luke some coins.

                    LUKE
        He says it's the best he can do. Since the
        XP-38 came out, they just aren't in demand.

                    BEN
        It will be enough.

Ben and Luke leave the speeder lot and walk down the dusty alleyway
past a small robot herding a bunch of anteater-like creatures. Luke
turns and gives one last forlorn look at his faithful speeder as he

                                              (CONTINUED)

SPECIAL EDITION INSERT TO PAGE 49

Suddenly the slimy alien fires his blaster at Han, hitting the wall just to the right of Han's head. In a blinding flash of light and smoke Greedo disappears as Han pulls his gun from beneath the table while the other patrons look on in bemused amazement. Han gets up and starts out of the cantina, flipping the bartender some coins as he leaves.

CONTINUED:

rounds a corner. A darkly clad creature moves out of the shadows as they pass and watches them as they disappear down another alley.

>BEN
>If the ship's as fast as he's boasting, we ought to do well.

INT. DOCKING BAY 94 — DAY

Jabba the Hutt and a half-dozen grisly alien pirates and purple creatures stand in the middle of the docking bay. Jabba is the grossest of the slavering hulks and his scarred face is a grim testimonial to his prowess as a vicious killer. He is a fat, slug-like creature with eyes on extended feelers and a huge ugly mouth.

>JABBA
>Come on out, Solo!

A voice from directly behind the pirates startles them and they turn around to see Han Solo and the giant Wookiee, Chewbacca, standing behind them with no weapons in sight.

>HAN
>I've been waiting for you, Jabba.

>JABBA
>I expected you would be.

>HAN
>I'm not the type to run.

>JABBA
>(fatherly-smooth) Han, my boy, there are times when you disappoint me . . . why haven't you paid me? And why did you have to fry poor Greedo like that . . . after all we've been through together.

>HAN
>You sent Greedo to blast me.

>JABBA
>(mock surprise) Han, why you're the best smuggler in the business. You're too valuable to fry. He was only relaying my concern at your delays. He wasn't going to blast you.

>HAN
>I think he thought he was. Next time don't send one of those twerps. If you've got something to say to me, come see me yourself.

CONTINUED:

                    JABBA
        Han, Han! If only you hadn't had to dump that
        shipment of spice . . . you understand I just
        can't make an exception. Where would I be if
        every pilot who smuggled for me dumped their
        shipment at the first sign of an Imperial
        starship? It's not good business.

                    HAN
        You know, even I get boarded sometimes,
        Jabba. I had no choice, but I've got a
        charter now and I can pay you back, plus a
        little extra. I just need some more time.

                    JABBA
        (to his men) Put your blasters away. Han, my
        boy, I'm only doing this because you're the
        best and I need you. So, for an extra,
        say . . . twenty percent I'll give you a
        little more time . . . but this is it. If you
        disappoint me again, I'll put a price on your
        head so large you won't be able to go near a
        civilized system for the rest of your short
        life.

                    HAN
        Jabba, I'll pay you because it's my pleasure.

EXT. DOCKING PORT ENTRY — ALLEYWAY

Chewbacca waits restlessly at the entrance to Docking Bay 94. Ben,
Luke, and the robots make their way up the street. Chewbacca jabbers
excitedly and signals for them to hurry. The darkly clad creature
has followed them from the speeder lot. He stops in a nearby doorway
and speaks into a small transmitter.

INT. MOS EISLEY SPACEPORT — DOCKING BAY 94

Chewbacca leads the group into the giant dirt pit that is Docking
Bay 94. Resting in the middle of the huge hole is a large, round,
beat-up, pieced-together hunk of junk that could only loosely be
called a starship.

                    LUKE
        What a piece of junk.

The tall figure of Han Solo comes down the boarding ramp.

                    HAN
        She'll make point five beyond the speed of
        light. She may not look like much, but she's
                    (MORE)

                                        (CONTINUED)

CONTINUED:

                    HAN (CONT'D)
          got it where it counts, kid. I've added some
          special modifications myself.

Luke scratches his head. It's obvious he isn't sure about all this.
Chewbacca rushes up the ramp and urges the others to follow.

                    HAN
          We're a little rushed, so if you'll hurry
          aboard we'll get out of here.

The group rushes up the gangplank, passing a grinning Han Solo.

INT. MILLENNIUM FALCON

Chewbacca settles into the pilot's chair and starts the mighty
engines of the starship.

INT. MOS EISLEY SPACEPORT — DOCKING BAY 94

Luke, Ben, Threepio, and Artoo move toward the <u>Millennium Falcon</u>
passing Solo.

                    THREEPIO
          Hello, sir.

EXT. TATOOINE — MOS EISLEY — STREET

Eight Imperial stormtroopers rush up to the darkly clad creature.

                    TROOPER
          Which way?

The darkly clad creature points to the door of the docking bay.

                    TROOPER
          All right, men. Load your weapons!

INT. MOS EISLEY SPACEPORT — DOCKING BAY 94

The troops hold their guns at the ready and charge down the docking
bay entrance.

                    TROOPER
          Stop that ship!

Han Solo looks up and sees the Imperial stormtroopers rushing into
the docking bay. Several of the troopers fire at Han as he ducks
into the spaceship.

(CONTINUED)

[54]

CONTINUED:

                         TROOPER
        Blast 'em!

Han draws his laser pistol and pops off a couple of shots which
force the stormtroopers to dive for safety. The pirateship engines
whine as Han hits the release button that slams the overhead entry
shut.

INT. MILLENNIUM FALCON

                         HAN
        Chewie, get us out of here!

The group straps in for takeoff.

                         THREEPIO
        Oh, my. I'd forgotten how much I hate space
        travel.

EXT. TATOOINE — MOS EISLEY — STREETS

The half-dozen stormtroopers at a check point hear the general alarm
and look to the sky as the huge starship rises above the dingy slum
dwellings and quickly disappears into the morning sky.

INT. MILLENNIUM FALCON — CABIN

Han climbs into the pilot's chair next to Chewbacca, who chatters
away as he points to something on the radar scope.

EXT. SPACE — PLANET TATOOINE

The Corellian pirateship zooms from Tatooine into space.

INT. MILLENNIUM FALCON — COCKPIT

Han frantically types information into the ship's computer. Little
Artoo appears momentarily at the cockpit doorway, makes a few
beeping remarks, then scurries away.

                         HAN
        It looks like an Imperial cruiser. Our
        passengers must be hotter than I thought. Try
        and hold them off. Angle the deflector shield
        while I make the calculations for the jump to
        lightspeed.

EXT. SPACE — PLANET TATOOINE

The <u>Millennium</u> <u>Falcon</u> pirateship races away from the yellow planet, Tatooine. It is followed by two huge Imperial Star Destroyers.

INT. MILLENNIUM FALCON — COCKPIT

Over the shoulders of Chewbacca and Han, we can see the galaxy spread before them. Luke and Ben make their way into the cramped cockpit where Han continues his calculation.

> HAN
> Stay sharp! There are two more coming in; they're going to try to cut us off.

> LUKE
> Why don't you outrun them? I thought you said this thing was fast.

> HAN
> Watch your mouth, kid, or you're going to find yourself floating home. We'll be safe enough once we make the jump to hyperspace. Besides, I know a few maneuvers. We'll lose them!

EXT. SPACE — PLANET TATOOINE

Imperial cruisers fire at the pirateship.

INT. MILLENNIUM FALCON — COCKPIT

The ship shudders as an explosion flashes outside the window.

> HAN
> Here's where the fun begins!

> BEN
> How long before you can make the jump to lightspeed?

> HAN
> It'll take a few moments to get the coordinates from the navi-computer.

The ship begins to rock violently as lasers hit it.

> LUKE
> Are you kidding? At the rate they're gaining . . .

(CONTINUED)

CONTINUED:

> HAN
>
> Traveling through hyperspace isn't like
> dusting crops, boy! Without precise calcula-
> tions we could fly right through a star or
> bounce too close to a supernova and that'd
> end your trip real quick, wouldn't it?

The ship is now constantly battered with laserfire as a red warning
light begins to flash.

> LUKE
>
> What's that flashing?

> HAN
>
> We're losing our deflector shield. Go strap
> yourself in, I'm going to make the jump to
> lightspeed.

The galaxy brightens and they move faster, almost as if crashing a
barrier. Stars become streaks as the pirateship makes the jump to
hyperspace.

EXT. SPACE

The Millennium Falcon zooms into infinity in less than a second.

EXT. DEATH STAR

Alderaan looms behind the Death Star battle station.

INT. DEATH STAR — CONTROL ROOM

Admiral Motti enters the quiet control room and bows before Governor
Tarkin, who stands before the huge wall screen displaying a small
green planet.

> MOTTI
>
> We've entered the Alderaan system.

Vader and two stormtroopers enter with Princess Leia. Her hands are
bound.

> LEIA
>
> Governor Tarkin, I should have expected to
> find you holding Vader's leash. I recognized
> your foul stench when I was brought on board.

> TARKIN
>
> Charming to the last. You don't know how hard
> I found it signing the order to terminate
> your life!

(CONTINUED)

CONTINUED:

                        LEIA
I'm surprised you had the courage to take the
responsibility yourself!

                        TARKIN
Princess Leia, before your execution I would
like you to be my guest at a ceremony that
will make this battle station operational. No
star system will dare oppose the Emperor now.

                        LEIA
The more you tighten your grip, Tarkin, the
more star systems will slip through your
fingers.

                        TARKIN
Not after we demonstrate the power of this
station. In a way, you have determined the
choice of the planet that'll be destroyed
first. Since you are reluctant to provide us
with the location of the Rebel base, I have
chosen to test this station's destructive
power . . . on your home planet of Alderaan.

                        LEIA
No! Alderaan is peaceful. We have no weapons.
You can't possibly . . .

                        TARKIN
You would prefer another target? A military
target? Then name the system!

Tarkin waves menacingly toward Leia.

                        TARKIN
I grow tired of asking this. So it'll be the
last time. Where is the Rebel base?

Leia overhears an intercom voice announcing the approach to
Alderaan.

                        LEIA
(softly) Dantooine.

Leia lowers her head.

                        LEIA
They're on Dantooine.

                        TARKIN
There. You see, Lord Vader, she can be
reasonable. (addressing Motti) Continue with
the operation. You may fire when ready.

                        LEIA
What?

                                            (CONTINUED)

CONTINUED:

                        TARKIN
        You're far too trusting. Dantooine is too
        remote to make an effective demonstration.
        But don't worry. We will deal with your Rebel
        friends soon enough.

                        LEIA

        No!

INT. DEATH STAR — BLAST CHAMBER

                        VADER
        Commence primary ignition.

A button is pressed which switches on a panel of lights. A hooded
Imperial soldier reaches overhead and pulls a lever. Another lever
is pulled. Vader reaches for still another lever and a bank of
lights on a panel and wall light up. A huge beam of light emanates
from within a cone-shaped area and converges into a single laser
beam out toward Alderaan. The small green planet of Alderaan is
blown into space dust.

INT. MILLENNIUM FALCON — CENTRAL HOLD AREA

Ben watches as Luke practices the lightsaber with a small "seeker"
robot. Ben suddenly turns away and sits down. He falters, seems
almost faint.

                        LUKE
        Are you all right? What's wrong?

                        BEN
        I felt a great disturbance in the Force . . .
        as if millions of voices suddenly cried out
        in terror and were suddenly silenced. I fear
        something terrible has happened.

Ben rubs his forehead. He seems to drift into a trance. Then he
fixes his gaze on Luke.

                        BEN
        You'd better get on with your exercises.

Han Solo enters the room.

                        HAN
        Well, you can forget your troubles with those
        Imperial slugs. I told you I'd outrun 'em.

Luke is once again practicing with the lightsaber.

                        HAN
        Don't everybody thank me at once.

CONTINUED:

Threepio watches Chewbacca and Artoo who are engrossed in a game in
which three-dimensional holographic figures move along a chess-type
board.

                    HAN
          Anyway, we should be at Alderaan about
          oh-two-hundred hours.

Chewbacca and the two robots sit around the lighted table covered
with small holographic monsters. Each side of the table has a small
computer monitor embedded in it. Chewbacca seems very pleased with
himself as he rests his lanky fur-covered arms over his head.

                    THREEPIO
          Now be careful, Artoo.

Artoo immediately reaches up and taps the computer with his stubby
claw hand, causing one of the holographic creatures to walk to the
new square. A sudden frown crosses Chewbacca's face and he begins
yelling gibberish at the tiny robot. Threepio intercedes on behalf
of his small companion and begins to argue with the huge Wookiee.

                    THREEPIO
          He made a fair move. Screaming about it won't
          help you.

                    HAN
          (interrupting) Let him have it. It's not wise
          to upset a Wookiee.

                    THREEPIO
          But sir, nobody worries about upsetting a
          droid.

                    HAN
          That's 'cause droids don't pull people's arms
          out of their sockets when they lose. Wookiees
          are known to do that.

                    THREEPIO
          I see your point, sir. I suggest a new
          strategy, Artoo. Let the Wookiee win.

Luke stands in the middle of the small hold area; he seems frozen in
place. A humming lightsaber is held high over his head. Ben watches
him from the corner, studying his movements. Han watches with a bit
of smugness.

                    BEN
          Remember, a Jedi can feel the Force flowing
          through him.

                    LUKE
          You mean it controls your actions?

                    BEN
          Partially. But it also obeys your commands.

                                        (CONTINUED)

CONTINUED:

Suspended at eye level, about ten feet in front of Luke, a "seeker,"
a chrome baseball-like robot covered with antennae, hovers slowly in
a wide arc. The ball floats to one side of the youth then to the
other. Suddenly it makes a lightning-swift lunge and stops within a
few feet of Luke's face. Luke doesn't move and the ball backs off.
It slowly moves behind the boy, then makes another quick lunge, this
time emitting a blood red laser beam as it attacks. It hits Luke in
the leg causing him to tumble over. Han lets loose with a burst of
laughter.

                    HAN
          Hokey religions and ancient weapons are no
          match for a good blaster at your side, kid.

                    LUKE
          You don't believe in the Force, do you?

                    HAN
          Kid, I've flown from one side of this galaxy
          to the other. I've seen a lot of strange
          stuff, but I've never seen anything to make
          me believe there's one all-powerful force
          controlling everything. There's no mystical
          energy field that controls my destiny.

Ben smiles quietly.

                    HAN
          It's all a lot of simple tricks and nonsense.

                    BEN
          I suggest you try it again, Luke.

Ben places a large helmet on Luke's head which covers his eyes.

                    BEN
          This time, let go of your conscious self and
          act on instinct.

                    LUKE
          (laughing) With the blast shield down, I
          can't even see. How am I supposed to fight?

                    BEN
          Your eyes can deceive you. Don't trust them.

Han skeptically shakes his head as Ben throws the seeker into the
air. The ball shoots straight up in the air, then drops like a rock.
Luke swings the lightsaber around blindly missing the seeker, which
fires off a laserbolt that hits Luke square on the seat of the
pants. He lets out a painful yell and attempts to hit the seeker.

                    BEN
          Stretch out with your feelings.

(CONTINUED)

CONTINUED:

Luke stands in one place, seemingly frozen. The seeker makes a dive at Luke and, incredibly, he manages to deflect the bolt. The ball ceases firing and moves back to its original position.

> BEN
> You see, you can do it.

> HAN
> I call it luck.

> BEN
> In my experience, there's no such thing as luck.

> HAN
> Look, going good against remotes is one thing. Going good against the living? That's something else.

Solo notices a small light flashing on the far side of the control panel.

> HAN
> Looks like we're coming up on Alderaan.

Han and Chewbacca head back to the cockpit.

> LUKE
> You know, I did feel something. I could almost see the remote.

> BEN
> That's good. You have taken your first step into a large world.

INT. DEATH STAR — CONFERENCE ROOM

Imperial Officer Cass stands before Governor Tarkin and the evil Dark Lord Darth Vader.

> TARKIN
> Yes.

> OFFICER CASS
> Our scout ships have reached Dantooine. They found the remains of a Rebel base, but they estimate that it has been deserted for some time. They are now conducting an extensive search of the surrounding systems.

> TARKIN
> She lied! She lied to us!

(CONTINUED)

CONTINUED:

> VADER
> I told you she would never consciously betray
> the Rebellion.

> TARKIN
> Terminate her . . . immediately!

EXT. HYPERSPACE

The pirateship is just coming out of hyperspace; a strange surreal
light show surrounds the ship.

INT. MILLENNIUM FALCON — COCKPIT

> HAN
> Stand by, Chewie, here we go. Cut in the
> sublight engines.

Han pulls back on a control lever. Outside the cockpit window stars
begin streaking past, seem to decrease in speed, then stop. Suddenly
the starship begins to shudder and violently shake about. Asteroids
begin to race toward them, battering the sides of the ship.

> HAN
> What the . . . ? Aw, we've come out of hyper-
> space into a meteor shower. Some kind of
> asteroid collision. It's not on any of the
> charts.

The giant Wookiee flips off several controls and seems very cool in
the emergency. Luke makes his way into the bouncing cockpit.

> LUKE
> What's going on?

> HAN
> Our position is correct, except . . . no
> Alderaan!

> LUKE
> What do you mean? Where is it?

> HAN
> That's what I'm trying to tell you, kid. It
> ain't there. It's been totally blown away.

> LUKE
> What? How?

Ben moves into the cockpit behind Luke as the ship begins to settle
down.

(CONTINUED)

CONTINUED:

                         BEN
          Destroyed . . . by the Empire!

                         HAN
          The entire starfleet couldn't destroy the
          whole planet. It'd take a thousand ships with
          more fire power than I've . . .

A signal light starts flashing on the control panel and a muffled
alarm starts humming.

                         HAN
          There's another ship coming in.

                         LUKE
          Maybe they know what happened.

                         BEN
          It's an Imperial fighter.

Chewbacca barks his concern. A huge explosion bursts outside the
cockpit window, shaking the ship violently. A tiny, finned Imperial
TIE fighter races past the cockpit window.

                         LUKE
          It followed us!

                         BEN
          No. It's a short range fighter.

                         HAN
          There aren't any bases around here. Where did
          it come from?

EXT. SPACE

The fighter races past the Corellian pirateship.

INT. MILLENNIUM FALCON — COCKPIT

                         LUKE
          It sure is leaving in a big hurry. If they
          identify us, we're in big trouble.

                         HAN
          Not if I can help it. Chewie . . . jam its
          transmissions.

                         BEN
          It'd be as well to let it go. It's too far
          out of range.

(CONTINUED)

CONTINUED:

                              HAN
          Not for long . . .

EXT. SPACE

The pirateship zooms over the camera and away into the vastness of
space after the Imperial TIE fighter.

INT. MILLENNIUM FALCON — COCKPIT

The tension mounts as the pirateship gains on the tiny fighter. In
the distance, one of the stars becomes brighter until it is obvious
that the TIE ship is heading for it. Ben stands behind Chewbacca.

                              BEN
          A fighter that size couldn't get this deep
          into space on its own.

                              LUKE
          Then he must have gotten lost, been part of a
          convoy or something . . .

                              HAN
          Well, he ain't going to be around long enough
          to tell anyone about us.

EXT. SPACE

The TIE fighter is losing ground to the larger pirateship as they
race toward camera and disappear overhead.

INT. MILLENNIUM FALCON — COCKPIT

The distant star can now be distinguished as a small moon or planet.

                              LUKE
          Look at him. He's heading for that small
          moon.

                              HAN
          I think I can get him before he gets
          there . . . he's almost in range.

The small moon begins to take on the appearance of a monstrous
spherical battle station.

                              BEN
          That's not a moon! It's a space station.

                                              (CONTINUED)

CONTINUED:

                        HAN
        It's too big to be a space station.

                        LUKE
        I have a very bad feeling about this.

                        BEN
        Turn the ship around!

                        HAN
        Yeah, I think you're right. Full reverse!
        Chewie, lock in the auxiliary power.

The pirateship shudders and the TIE fighter accelerates away toward
the gargantuan battle station.

                        LUKE
        Why are we still moving toward it?

                        HAN
        We're caught in a tractor beam! It's pulling
        us in.

                        LUKE
        But there's gotta be something you can do!

                        HAN
        There's nothin' I can do about it, kid. I'm
        in full power. I'm going to have to shut
        down. But they're not going to get me without
        a fight!

Ben Kenobi puts a hand on his shoulder.

                        BEN
        You can't win. But there are alternatives to
        fighting.

INT. MILLENNIUM FALCON — DEATH STAR

As the battered starship is towed closer to the awesome metal moon,
the immense size of the massive battle station becomes staggering.
Running along the equator of the gigantic sphere is a mile-high band
of huge docking ports into which the helpless pirateship is dragged.

EXT. DEATH STAR — HUGE PORT DOORS

The helpless Millennium Falcon is pulled past a docking port control
room and huge laser turret cannons.

                VOICE OVER DEATH STAR INTERCOM
        Clear Bay twenty-three-seven. We are opening
        the magnetic field.

INT. DEATH STAR — DOCKING BAY 2037

The pirateship is pulled in through port doors of the Death Star,
coming to rest in a huge hangar. Thirty stormtroopers stand at
attention in a central assembly area.

>   OFFICER
>   To your stations! (to another officer) Come
>   with me.

INT. DEATH STAR — HALLWAY

Stormtroopers run to their posts.

INT. DEATH STAR — HANGAR 2037

A line of stormtroopers march toward the pirateship in readiness to
board it, while other troopers stand with weapons ready to fire.

>   OFFICER
>   Close all outboard shields! Close all
>   outboard shields!

INT. DEATH STAR — CONFERENCE ROOM

Tarkin pushes a button and responds to intercom buzz.

>   TARKIN
>   Yes.

>   VOICE
>   (over intercom) We've captured a freighter
>   entering the remains of the Alderaan system.
>   Its markings match those of a ship that
>   blasted its way out of Mos Eisley.

>   VADER
>   They must be trying to return the stolen
>   plans to the princess. She may yet be of some
>   use to us.

INT. DEATH STAR — DOCKING BAY 2037

Vader and a commander approach the troops as an officer and several
heavily armed troops exit the spacecraft.

>   VOICE
>   (over intercom) Unlock one-five-seven and
>   nine. Release charges.

(CONTINUED)

CONTINUED:

                          OFFICER
          (to Vader) There's no one on board, sir.
          According to the log, the crew abandoned ship
          right after takeoff. It must be a decoy, sir.
          Several of the escape pods have been
          jettisoned.

                          VADER
          Did you find any droids?

                          OFFICER
          No, sir. If there were any on board, they
          must also have jettisoned.

                          VADER
          Send a scanning crew on board. I want every
          part of this ship checked.

                          OFFICER
          Yes, sir.

                          VADER
          I sense something . . . a presence I haven't
          felt since . . .

Vader turns quickly and exits the hangar.

                          OFFICER
          Get me a scanning crew in here on the double.
          I want every part of this ship checked!

INT. MILLENNIUM FALCON — HALLWAY

A trooper runs through the hallway heading for the exit. In a few
moments all is quiet. The muffled sounds of a distant officer giving
orders finally fade. Two floor panels suddenly pop up revealing Han
Solo and Luke. Ben Kenobi sticks his head out of a third locker.

                          LUKE
          Boy, it's lucky you had these compartments.

                          HAN
          I use them for smuggling. I never thought I'd
          be smuggling myself in them. This is ridicu-
          lous. Even if I could take off, I'd never get
          past the tractor beam.

                          BEN
          Leave that to me!

                          HAN
          Damn fool. I knew that you were going to say
          that!

CONTINUED:

                          BEN
          Who's the more foolish . . . the fool or the
          fool who follows him?

Han shakes his head, muttering to himself. Chewbacca agrees.

INT. DEATH STAR — MAIN FORWARD BAY

The two crewmen carry a heavy box on board the ship, past the two
stormtroopers guarding either side of the ramp.

                          TROOPER
          The ship's all yours. If the scanners pick up
          anything, report it immediately. All right,
          let's go.

The crewmen enter the pirateship and a loud crashing sound is
followed by a voice calling to the guard below.

                          HAN'S VOICE
          Hey down there, could you give us a hand with
          this?

The stormtroopers enter the ship and a quick round of gunfire is
heard.

INT. DEATH STAR — FORWARD BAY — COMMAND OFFICE

In a very small command office near the entrance to the pirateship,
a gantry officer looks out his window and notices the guards are
missing. He speaks into the comlink.

                          GANTRY OFFICER
          TX-four-two-one. Why aren't you at your post?
          TX-four-two-one, do you copy?

A stormtrooper comes down the ramp of the pirateship and waves to
the gantry officer, pointing to his ear indicating his comlink is
not working. The gantry officer shakes his head in disgust and heads
for the door, giving his aide an annoyed look.

                          GANTRY OFFICER
          Take over. We've got a bad transmitter. I'll
          see what I can do.

As the officer approaches the door, it slides open revealing the
towering Chewbacca. The gantry officer, in a momentary state of
shock, stumbles backward. With a bone-chilling howl, the giant
Wookiee flattens the officer with one blow. The aide immediately
reaches for his pistol, but is blasted by Han, dressed as an
Imperial stormtrooper. Ben and the robots enter the room quickly
followed by Luke, also dressed as a stormtrooper. Luke quickly
removes his helmet.

                                              (CONTINUED)

The Death Star's only weakness lay in an exhaust port at the end of a narrow trench, heavily guarded by cannon emplacements.

The destruction of the Death Star was most spectacular.

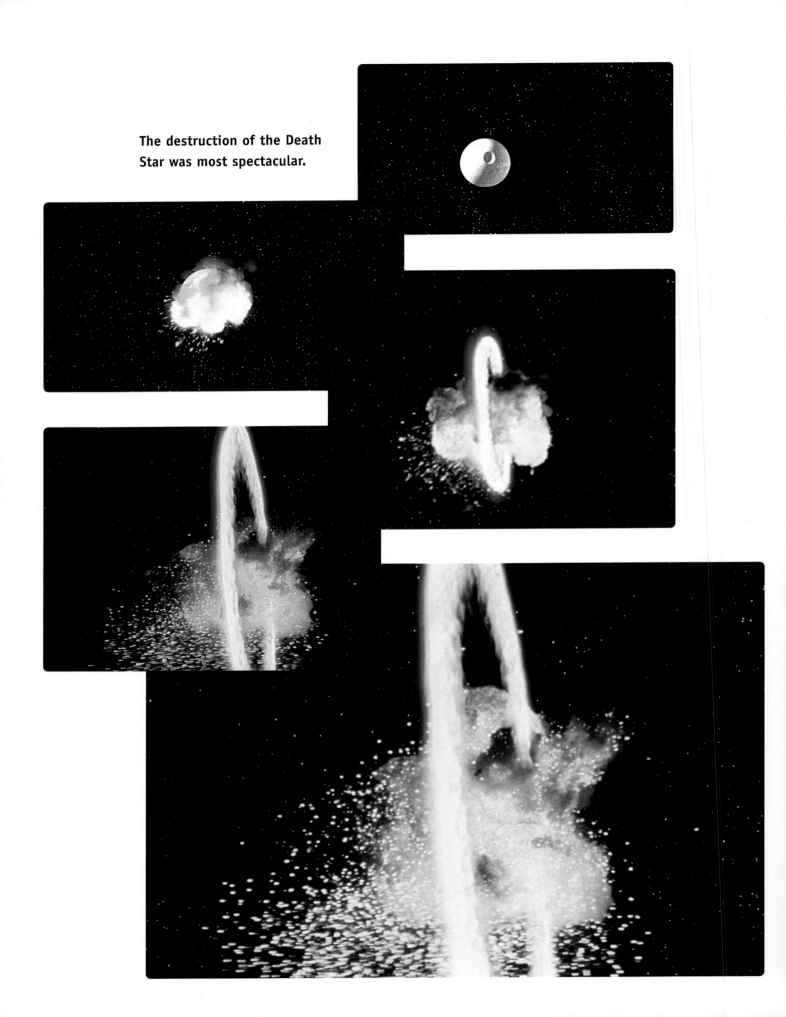

CONTINUED:

>   LUKE
>   You know, between his howling and your
>   blasting everything in sight, it's a wonder
>   the whole station doesn't know we're here.

>   HAN
>   Bring them on! I prefer a straight fight to
>   all this sneaking around.

>   THREEPIO
>   We found the computer outlet, sir.

Ben feeds some information into the computer and a map of the city
appears on the monitor. He begins to inspect it carefully. Threepio
and Artoo look over the control panel. Artoo finds something that
makes him whistle wildly.

>   BEN
>   Plug in. He should be able to interpret the
>   entire Imperial computer network.

Artoo punches his claw arm into the computer socket and the vast
Imperial brain network comes to life, feeding information to the
little robot. After a few moments, he beeps something.

>   THREEPIO
>   He says he's found the main control to the
>   power beam that's holding the ship here.
>   He'll try to make the precise location appear
>   on the monitor.

The computer monitor flashes readouts.

>   THREEPIO
>   The tractor beam is coupled to the main
>   reactor in seven locations. A power loss at
>   one of the terminals will allow the ship to
>   leave.

Ben studies the data on the monitor readout.

>   BEN
>   I don't think you boys can help. I must go
>   alone.

>   HAN
>   Whatever you say. I've done more than I
>   bargained for on this trip already.

>   LUKE
>   I want to go with you.

>   BEN
>   Be patient, Luke. Stay and watch over the
>   droids.

CONTINUED:

                    LUKE
        But he can . . .

                    BEN
        They must be delivered safely or other star
        systems will suffer the same fate as
        Alderaan. Your destiny lies along a different
        path from mine. The Force will be with
        you . . . always!

Ben adjusts the lightsaber on his belt and silently steps out of the
command office, then disappears down a long gray hallway. Chewbacca
barks a comment and Han shakes his head in agreement.

                    HAN
        Boy, you said it, Chewie.

Han looks at Luke.

                    HAN
        Where did you dig up that old fossil?

                    LUKE
        Ben is a great man.

                    HAN
        Yeah, great at getting us into trouble.

                    LUKE
        I didn't hear you give any ideas . . .

                    HAN
        Well, anything would be better than just
        hanging around waiting for them to pick us
        up . . .

                    LUKE
        Why do you think . . .

Suddenly Artoo begins to whistle and beep a blue streak. Luke goes
over to him.

                    LUKE
        What is it?

                    THREEPIO
        I'm afraid I'm not quite sure, sir. He says
        "I found her," and keeps repeating, "She's
        here."

                    LUKE
        Well, who . . . who has he found?

Artoo whistles a frantic reply.

                    THREEPIO
        Princess Leia.

CONTINUED:

                    LUKE
    The princess? She's here?

                    HAN
    Princess?

                    LUKE
    Where . . . where is she?

                    HAN
    Princess? What's going on?

                    THREEPIO
    Level five. Detention block AA-twenty-three.
    I'm afraid she's scheduled to be terminated.

                    LUKE
    Oh, no! We've got to do something.

                    HAN
    What are you talking about?

                    LUKE
    The droid belongs to her. She's the one in
    the message. We've got to help her.

                    HAN
    Now, look, don't get any funny ideas. The old
    man wants us to wait right here.

                    LUKE
    But he didn't know she was here. Look, will
    you just find a way back into that detention
    block?

                    HAN
    I'm not going anywhere.

                    LUKE
    They're going to execute her. Look, a few
    minutes ago you said you didn't want to just
    wait here to be captured. Now all you want to
    do is stay.

                    HAN
    Marching into the detention area is not what
    I had in mind.

                    LUKE
    But they're going to kill her!

                    HAN
    Better her than me . . .

                    LUKE
    She's rich.

Chewbacca growls.

CONTINUED:

                    HAN
        Rich?

                    LUKE
        Yes. Rich, powerful! Listen, if you were to
        rescue her, the reward would be . . .

                    HAN
        What?

                    LUKE
        Well, more wealth than you can imagine.

                    HAN
        I don't know, I can imagine quite a bit!

                    LUKE
        You'll get it!

                    HAN
        I'd better!

                    LUKE
        You will . . .

                    HAN
        All right, kid. But you'd better be right
        about this!

Han looks at Chewie, who grunts a short grunt.

                    LUKE
        All right.

                    HAN
        What's your plan?

                    LUKE
        Uh . . . Threepio, hand me those binders
        there will you?

Luke moves toward Chewbacca with electronic cuffs.

                    LUKE
        Okay. Now, I'm going to put these on you.

Chewie lets out a hideous growl.

                    LUKE
        Okay. Han, you put these on.

Luke sheepishly hands the binders to Han.

                    HAN
        Don't worry, Chewie. I think I know what he
        has in mind.

The Wookiee has a worried and frightened look on his face as Han
binds him with electronic cuffs.

(CONTINUED)

CONTINUED:

                    THREEPIO
        Master Luke, sir! Pardon me for asking . . .
        but, ah . . . what should Artoo and I do if
        we're discovered here?

                    LUKE
        Lock the door!

                    HAN
        And hope they don't have blasters.

                    THREEPIO
        That isn't very reassuring.

Luke and Han put on their armored stormtrooper helmets and start off
into the giant Imperial Death Star.

INT. DEATH STAR - DETENTION AREA - ELEVATOR TUBE

Han and Luke try to look inconspicuous in their armored suits as
they wait for a vacuum elevator to arrive. Troops, bureaucrats, and
robots bustle about, ignoring the trio completely. Only a few give
the giant Wookiee a curious glance.

Finally a small elevator arrives and the trio enters.

                    LUKE
        I can't see a thing in this helmet.

A bureaucrat races to get aboard also, but is signaled away by Han.
The door to the pod-like vehicle slides closed and the elevator car
takes off through a vacuum tube.

INT. DEATH STAR - MAIN HALLWAY

Several Imperial officers walk through the wide main passageway.
They pass several stormtroopers and a robot similar to Threepio but
with an insect face. At the far end of the hallway, a passing flash
of Ben Kenobi appears, then disappears down a small hallway. His
appearance is so fleeting that it is hard to tell if he is real or
just an illusion. No one in the hallway seems to notice him.

INT. DEATH STAR - INTERIOR ELEVATOR - DETENTION SECURITY AREA

Luke and Han step forward to exit the elevator, but the door slides
open behind them. The giant Wookiee and his two guards enter the old
gray security station. Guards and laser gates are everywhere. Han
whispers to Luke under his breath.

                    HAN
        This is not going to work.

                                            (CONTINUED)

CONTINUED:

                              LUKE
          Why didn't you say so before?

                              HAN
          I did say so before!

INT. DETENTION AREA

Elevator doors open. A tall, grim-looking officer approaches
the trio.

                              OFFICER
          Where are you taking this . . . thing?

Chewie growls a bit at the remark but Han nudges him to shut up.

                              LUKE
          Prisoner transfer from Block one-one-three-
          eight.

                              OFFICER
          I wasn't notified. I'll have to clear it.

The officer goes back to his console and begins to punch in the
information. There are only three other troopers in the area. Luke
and Han survey the situation, checking all of the alarms, laser
gates, and camera eyes. Han unfastens one of Chewbacca's electronic
cuffs and shrugs to Luke.

Suddenly Chewbacca throws up his hands and lets out with one of his
ear-piercing howls. He grabs Han's laser rifle.

                              HAN
          Look out! He's loose!

                              LUKE
          He's going to pull us all apart!

                              HAN
          Go get him!

The startled guards are momentarily dumbfounded. Luke and Han have
already pulled out their laser pistols and are blasting away at the
terrifying Wookiee. Their barrage of laserfire misses Chewbacca, but
hits the camera eyes, laser gate controls, and the Imperial guards.
The officer is the last of the guards to fall under the laserfire
just as he is about to push the alarm system. Han rushes to the
comlink system, which is screeching questions about what is going
on. He quickly checks the computer readout.

                              HAN
          We've got to find out which cell this
          princess of yours is in. Here it is . . .
                          (MORE)

(CONTINUED)

CONTINUED:

                    HAN (CONT'D)
          cell twenty-one-eight-seven. You go get her.
          I'll hold them here.

Luke races down one of the cell corridors. Han speaks into the
buzzing comlink.

                    HAN
          (sounding official) Everything is under
          control. Situation normal.

                    INTERCOM VOICE
          What happened?

                    HAN
          (getting nervous) Uh . . . had a slight
          weapons malfunction. But, uh, everything's
          perfectly all right now. We're fine. We're
          all fine here, now, thank you. How are you?

                    INTERCOM VOICE
          We're sending a squad up.

                    HAN
          Uh, uh, negative, negative. We had a reactor
          leak here now. Give us a few minutes to lock
          it down. Large leak . . . very dangerous.

                    INTERCOM VOICE
          Who is this? What's your operating number?

Han blasts the comlink and it explodes.

                    HAN
          Boring conversation anyway. (yelling down the
          hall) Luke! We're going to have company!

INT. DEATH STAR — CELL ROW

Luke stops in front of one of the cells and blasts the door away
with his laser pistol. When the smoke clears, Luke sees the dazzling
young princess-senator. She had been sleeping and is now looking at
him with an uncomprehending look on her face. Luke is stunned by her
incredible beauty and stands staring at her with his mouth hanging
open.

                    LEIA
          (finally) Aren't you a little short for a
          stormtrooper?

Luke takes off his helmet, coming out of it.

                    LUKE
          What? Oh . . . the uniform. I'm Luke
          Skywalker. I'm here to rescue you.

                                                        (CONTINUED)

CONTINUED:

                    LEIA
    You're who?

                    LUKE
    I'm here to rescue you. I've got your R2
    unit. I'm here with Ben Kenobi.

                    LEIA
    Ben Kenobi is here! Where is he?

                    LUKE
    Come on!

INT. DEATH STAR — CONFERENCE ROOM

Darth Vader paces the room as Governor Tarkin sits at the far end of
the conference table.

                    VADER
    He is here . . .

                    TARKIN
    Obi-Wan Kenobi! What makes you think so?

                    VADER
    A tremor in the Force. The last time I felt
    it was in the presence of my old master.

                    TARKIN
    Surely he must be dead by now.

                    VADER
    Don't underestimate the Force.

                    TARKIN
    The Jedi are extinct, their fire has gone out
    of the universe. You, my friend, are all
    that's left of their religion.

There is a quiet buzz on the comlink.

                    TARKIN
    Yes.

                    INTERCOM VOICE
    Governor Tarkin, we have an emergency alert
    in detention block AA-twenty-three.

                    TARKIN
    The princess! Put all sections on alert!

                    VADER
    Obi-Wan _is_ here. The Force is with him.

                    TARKIN
    If you're right, he must not be allowed to
    escape.

CONTINUED:

                          VADER
          Escape may not be his plan. I must face him
          alone.

INT. DEATH STAR — DETENTION AREA — HALLWAY

An ominous buzzing sound is heard on the other side of the elevator
door.

                          HAN
              Chewie!

Chewbacca responds with a growling noise.

                          HAN
              Get behind me! Get behind me!

A series of explosions knocks a hole in the elevator door through
which several Imperial troops begin to emerge.

Han and Chewie fire their laser pistols at them through the smoke
and flames. They turn and run down the cell hallway, meeting up with
Luke and Leia rushing toward them.

                          HAN
              Can't get out that way.

                          LEIA
              Looks like you managed to cut off our only
              escape route.

                          HAN
              (sarcastically) Maybe you'd like it back in
              your cell, Your Highness.

Luke takes a small comlink transmitter from his belt as they
continue to exchange fire with stormtroopers making their way down
the corridor.

                          LUKE
              See-Threepio! See-Threepio!

                          THREEPIO
              (over comlink) Yes sir?

                          LUKE
              We've been cut off! Are there any other ways
              out of the cell bay? . . . What was that? I
              didn't copy!

INT. DEATH STAR — MAIN BAY GANTRY — CONTROL TOWER

Threepio paces the control center as little Artoo beeps and whistles
a blue streak. Threepio yells into the small comlink transmitter.

CONTINUED:

                    THREEPIO
        I said, all systems have been alerted to your
        presence, sir. The main entrance seems to be
        the only way in or out; all other information
        on your level is restricted.

Someone begins banging on the door.

                    TROOPER VOICE
        Open up in there!

                    THREEPIO
        Oh, no!

INT. DEATH STAR — DETENTION CORRIDOR

Luke and Leia crouch together in an alcove for protection as they
continue to exchange fire with troops. Han and Chewbacca are barely
able to keep the stormtroopers at bay at the far end of the hallway.
The laserfire is very intense, and smoke fills the narrow cell
corridor.

                    LUKE
        There isn't any other way out.

                    HAN
        I can't hold them off forever! Now what?

                    LEIA
        This is some rescue. When you came in here,
        didn't you have a plan for getting out?

                    HAN
        (pointing to Luke) He is the brains,
        sweetheart.

Luke manages a sheepish grin and shrugs his shoulders.

                    LUKE
        Well, I didn't . . .

The princess grabs Luke's gun and fires at a small grate in the wall
next to Han, almost frying him.

                    HAN
        What the hell are you doing?

                    LEIA
        Somebody has to save our skins. Into the
        garbage chute, wise guy.

She jumps through the narrow opening as Han and Chewbacca look on in
amazement. Chewbacca sniffs the garbage chute and says something.

                    HAN
        Get in there you big furry oaf! I don't care
                    (MORE)

                                                    (CONTINUED)

CONTINUED:

                    HAN (CONT'D)
          what you smell! Get in there and don't worry
          about it.

Han gives him a big kick and the Wookiee disappears into the tiny
opening. Luke and Han continue firing as they work their way toward
the opening.

                    HAN
          Wonderful girl! Either I'm going to kill her
          or I'm beginning to like her. Get in there!

Luke ducks laserfire as he jumps into the darkness. Han fires off a
couple of quick blasts creating a smoky cover, then slides into the
chute himself and is gone.

INT. DEATH STAR — GARBAGE ROOM

Han tumbles into a large room filled with garbage and muck. Luke is
already stumbling around looking for an exit. He finds a small
hatchway and struggles to get it open. It won't budge.

                    HAN
          (sarcastically) Oh! The garbage chute was a
          really wonderful idea. What an incredible
          smell you've discovered! Let's get out of
          here! Get away from there . . .
                    LUKE
          No! Wait!

Han draws his laser pistol and fires at the hatch. The laserbolt
ricochets wildly around the small metal room. Everyone dives for
cover in the garbage as the bolt explodes almost on top of them.
Leia climbs out of the garbage with a rather grim look on her face.

                    LUKE
          Will you forget it? I already tried it. It's
          magnetically sealed!
                    LEIA
          Put that thing away! You're going to get us
          all killed.
                    HAN
          Absolutely, Your Worship. Look, I had every-
          thing under control until you led us down
          here. You know, it's not going to take them
          long to figure out what happened to us.
                    LEIA
          It could be worse . . .

A loud, horrible, inhuman moan works its way up from the murky

CONTINUED:

depths. Chewbacca lets out a terrified howl and begins to back away. Han and Luke stand fast with their laser pistols drawn. The Wookiee is cowering near one of the walls.

                    HAN
          It's worse.

                    LUKE
          There's something alive in here!

                    HAN
          That's your imagination.

                    LUKE
          Something just moved past my leg! Look! Did
          you see that?

                    HAN
          What?

                    LUKE
          Help!

Suddenly Luke is yanked under the garbage.

                    HAN
          Luke! Luke! Luke!

Solo tries to get to Luke. Luke surfaces with a gasp of air and thrashing of limbs. A membrane tentacle is wrapped around his throat.

                    LEIA
          Luke!

Leia extends a long pipe toward him.

                    LEIA
          Luke, Luke, grab a hold of this.

                    LUKE
          Blast it, will you! My gun's jammed.

                    HAN
          Where?

                    LUKE
          Anywhere. Oh!!

Solo fires his gun downward. Luke is pulled back into the muck by the slimy tentacle.

                    HAN
          Luke! Luke!

Suddenly the walls of the garbage receptacle shudder and move in a couple of inches. Then everything is deathly quiet. Han and Leia give each other a worried look as Chewbacca howls in the corner. With a rush of bubbles and muck Luke suddenly bobs to the surface.

                                        (CONTINUED)

CONTINUED:

                              LEIA
               Grab him!

Luke seems to be released by the thing.

                              LEIA
               What happened?

                              LUKE
               I don't know, it just let go of me and
               disappeared . . .

                              HAN
               I've got a very bad feeling about this.

Before anyone can say anything the walls begin to rumble and edge
toward the Rebels.

                              LUKE
               The walls are moving!

                              LEIA
               Don't just stand there. Try and brace it with
               something.

They place poles and long metal beams between the closing walls, but
they are simply snapped and bent as the giant trashmasher rumbles
on. The situation doesn't look too good.

                              LUKE
               Wait a minute!

Luke pulls out his comlink.

                              LUKE
               Threepio! Come in Threepio! Threepio! Where
               could he be?

INT. DEATH STAR — MAIN GANTRY — COMMAND OFFICE

A soft buzzer and the muted voice of Luke calling out for See-
Threepio can be heard on Threepio's hand comlink, which is siting on
the deserted computer console. Artoo and Threepio are nowhere in
sight. Suddenly there is a great explosion and the door of the
control tower flies across the floor. Four armed stormtroopers enter
the chamber.

                         FIRST TROOPER
               Take over! (pointing to a dead officer) See
               to him! Look there!

A trooper pushes a button and the supply cabinet door slides open.
See-Threepio and Artoo-Detoo are inside. Artoo follows his bronze
companion out into the office.

                                                    (CONTINUED)

CONTINUED:

                    THREEPIO
        They're madmen! They're heading for the
        prison level. If you hurry, you might catch
        them.

                    FIRST OFFICER
        (to his troops) Follow me! You stand guard.

The troops hustle off down the hallway, leaving the guard to watch
over the command office.

                    THREEPIO
        (to Artoo) Come on!

The guard aims a blaster at them.

                    THREEPIO
        Oh! All this excitement has overrun the
        circuits in my counterpart here. If you
        don't mind, I'd like to take him down to
        maintenance.

                    TROOPER
        All right.

The guard nods and Threepio, with little Artoo in tow, hurries out
the door.

INT. DEATH STAR — GARBAGE ROOM

As the walls rumble closer, the room gets smaller and smaller.
Chewie is whining and trying to hold a wall back with his giant
paws. Han is leaning back against the other wall. Garbage is
snapping and popping. Luke is trying to reach Threepio.

                    LUKE
        Threepio! Come in, Threepio! Threepio!

Han and Leia try to brace the contracting walls with a pole. Leia
begins to sink into the trash.

                    HAN
        Get to the top!

                    LEIA
        I can't.

                    LUKE
        Where could he be? Threepio! Threepio, will
        you come in?

                                              (CONTINUED)

INT. DEATH STAR — MAIN FORWARD BAY — SERVICE PANEL

> THREEPIO
> They aren't here! Something must have happened
> to them. See if they've been captured.

Little Artoo carefully plugs his claw arm into a new wall socket and
a complex array of electronic sounds spew from the tiny robot.

> THREEPIO
> Hurry!

INT. DEATH STAR — GARBAGE ROOM

The walls are only feet apart. Leia and Han are braced against the
walls. The princess is frightened. They look at each other. Leia
reaches out and takes Han's hand and holds it tightly. She's terrified and suddenly groans as she feels the first crushing pressure
against her body.

> HAN
> One thing's for sure. We're all going to be a
> lot thinner! (to Leia) Get on top of it!

> LEIA
> I'm trying!

INT. DEATH STAR — MAIN FORWARD BAY — SERVICE PANEL

> THREEPIO
> (to Artoo) Thank goodness, they haven't found
> them! Where could they be?

Artoo frantically beeps something to See-Threepio.

> THREEPIO
> Use the comlink? Oh, my! I forgot I turned it
> off!

INT. DEATH STAR — GARBAGE ROOM

Meanwhile, Luke is lying on his side, trying to keep his head above the
rising ooze. Luke's comlink begins to buzz and he rips it off his belt.

INT. DEATH STAR — MAIN FORWARD BAY — SERVICE PANEL

Muffled sounds of Luke's voice over comlink can be heard, but not
distinctly.

> THREEPIO
> Are you there, sir?

(CONTINUED)

INT. DEATH STAR — GARBAGE ROOM

> LUKE
>
> Threepio!

INT. DEATH STAR — MAIN FORWARD BAY

> THREEPIO
> We've had some problems . . .
>
> LUKE
> (over comlink) Will you shut up and listen to
> me? Shut down all garbage mashers on the
> detention level, will you? Do you copy?

INT. DEATH STAR — GARBAGE ROOM

> LUKE
>
> Shut down all the garbage mashers on the
> detention level.

INT. DEATH STAR — MAIN FORWARD BAY — SERVICE PANEL

> LUKE
> (over comlink) Shut down all the garbage
> mashers on the detention level.
>
> THREEPIO
> (to Artoo) No. Shut them all down! Hurry!

Threepio holds his head in agony as he hears the incredible screaming and hollering from Luke's comlink.

> THREEPIO
> Listen to them! They're dying, Artoo! Curse
> my metal body! I wasn't fast enough. It's all
> my fault! My poor master!
>
> LUKE
> (over comlink) Threepio, we're all right!

INT. DEATH STAR — GARBAGE ROOM

The screaming and hollering is the sound of joyous relief. The walls
have stopped moving. Han, Chewie, and Leia embrace in the
background.

> LUKE
> We're all right. You did great.

(CONTINUED)

CONTINUED:

Luke moves to the pressure sensitive hatch, looking for a number.

                    LUKE
          Hey . . . hey, open the pressure maintenance
          hatch on unit number . . . where are we?

INT. DEATH STAR — MAIN FORWARD BAY — SERVICE PANEL

Threepio looks at the computer panel as Han reads the number.

                    HAN:
          (over comlink) Three-two-six-eight-two-seven.

INT. DEATH STAR — TRACTOR BEAM — POWER GENERATOR TRENCH

Ben enters a humming service trench that powers the huge tractor
beam. The trench seems to be a hundred miles deep. The clacking
sound of huge switching devices can be heard. The old Jedi edges his
way along a narrow ledge leading to a control panel that connects
two large cables. He carefully makes several adjustments in the
computer terminal, and several lights on the board go from red to
blue.

INT. DEATH STAR — UNUSED HALLWAY

The group exits the garbage room into a dusty, unused hallway. Han
and Luke remove the trooper suits and strap on the blaster belts.

                    HAN
          If we can just avoid any more female advice,
          we ought to be able to get out of here.

Luke smiles and scratches his head as he takes a blaster from Solo.

                    LUKE
          Well, let's get moving!

Chewie begins growling and points to the hatch to the garbage room,
as he runs away and then stops howling.

                    HAN
          (to Chewie) Where are you going?

The dianoga bangs against the hatch and a long, slimy tentacle works
its way out of the doorway searching for a victim. Han aims his
pistol.

                    LEIA
          No, wait. They'll hear!

Han fires at the doorway. The noise of the blast echoes relentlessly

(CONTINUED)

CONTINUED:

throughout the empty passageway. Luke simply shakes his head in disgust.

> HAN
> (to Chewie) Come here, you big coward!

Chewie shakes his head "no."

> HAN
> Chewie! Come here!

> LEIA
> Listen. I don't know who you are, or where you come from, but from now on, you do as I tell you. Okay?

Han is stunned at the command of the petite young girl.

> HAN
> Look, Your Worshipfulness, let's get one thing straight! I take orders from one person! Me!

> LEIA
> It's a wonder you're still alive. (looking at Chewie) Will somebody get this big walking carpet out of my way?

Han watches her start away. He looks at Luke.

> HAN
> No reward is worth this.

They follow her, moving swiftly down the deserted corridor.

INT. DEATH STAR — POWER TRENCH

Suddenly a door behind Ben slides open and a detachment of stormtroopers marches to the power trench. Ben instantly slips into the shadows as an officer moves to within a few feet of him.

> OFFICER
> Secure this entry area until the alert is cancelled.

> FIRST TROOPER
> Give me regular reports.

All but two of the stormtroopers leave.

> FIRST TROOPER
> Do you know what's going on?

> SECOND TROOPER
> Maybe it's another drill.

Ben moves around the tractor beam, watching the stormtroopers as

CONTINUED:

they turn their backs to him. Ben gestures with his hand toward
them, as the troops think they hear something in the other hallway.
With the help of the Force, Ben deftly slips past the troopers and
into the main hallway.

                    SECOND TROOPER
          What was that?

                    FIRST TROOPER
          Oh, it's nothing. Don't worry about it.

INT. DEATH STAR — HALLWAY

Luke, Han, Chewbacca, and Leia run down an empty hallway and stop
before a bay window overlooking the pirateship. Troopers are milling
around the ship. Luke takes out his pocket comlink.

                    HAN
          (looking at his ship) There she is.

                    LUKE
          See-Threepio, do you copy?

                    THREEPIO
          (voice) For the moment. Uh, we're in the main
          hangar across from the ship.

                    LUKE
          We're right above you. Stand by.

Han is watching the dozen or so troops moving in and out of the
pirateship. Leia moves toward Han, touches his arm, and points out
the window to the ship.

                    LEIA
          You came in that thing? You're braver than I
          thought.

                    HAN
          Nice! Come on!

Han gives her a dirty look, and they start off down the hallway.
They round a corner and run right into twenty Imperial stormtroopers
heading toward them. Both groups are taken by surprise and stop in
their tracks.

                    FIRST TROOPER
          It's them! Blast them!

Before even thinking, Han draws his laser pistol and charges the
troops, firing. His blast knocks one of the stormtroopers into the
air. Chewie follows his captain down the corridor, stepping over
the fallen trooper on the floor.

                    HAN
          (to Luke and Leia) Get back to the ship!

                                                      (CONTINUED)

CONTINUED:

                         LUKE
          Where are you going? Come back!

Han has already rounded a corner and does not hear.

                         LEIA
          He certainly has courage.

                         LUKE
          What good will it do us if he gets himself
          killed? Come on!

Luke is furious but doesn't have time to think about it for muted
alarms begin to go off down on the hangar deck. Luke and Leia start
off toward the starship hangar.

INT. DEATH STAR — SUBHALLWAY

Han chases the stormtroopers down a long subhallway. He is yelling
and brandishing his laser pistol. The troops reach a dead end and
are forced to turn and fight. Han stops a few feet from them and
assumes a defensive position. The troops begin to raise their laser
guns. Soon all ten troopers are moving into an attack position in
front of the lone starpirate. Han's determined look begins to fade
as the troops begin to advance. Solo jumps backward as they fire at
him.

INT. DEATH STAR — SUBHALLWAY

Chewbacca runs down the subhallway in a last-ditch attempt to save
his bold captain. Suddenly he hears the firing of laser guns and
yelling. Around the corner shoots Han, pirate extraordinaire,
running for his life, followed by a host of furious stormtroopers.
Chewbacca turns and starts running the other way also.

INT. DEATH STAR — HALLWAY

Luke fires his laser pistol wildly as he and Leia rush down a narrow
subhallway, chased by several stormtroopers. They quickly reach the
end of the subhallway and race through an open hatchway.

INT. DEATH STAR — CENTRAL CORE SHAFT

Luke and Leia race through the hatch onto a narrow bridge that spans
a huge, deep shaft that seems to go into infinity. The bridge has
been retracted into the wall of the shaft, and Luke almost rushes
into the abyss. He loses his balance off the end of the bridge as
Leia, behind him, takes hold of his arm and pulls him back.

                                                    (CONTINUED)

CONTINUED:

                    LUKE
        (gasping) I think we took a wrong turn.

Blasts from the stormtroopers' laser guns explode nearby reminding
them of the oncoming danger. Luke fires back at the advancing
troops. Leia reaches over and hits a switch that pops the hatch door
shut with a resounding boom, leaving them precariously perched on a
short piece of bridge overhang. Laserfire from the troopers continues to hit the steel door.

                    LEIA
        There's no lock!

Luke blasts the controls with his laser pistol.

                    LUKE
        That oughta hold it for a while.

                    LEIA
        Quick, we've got to get across. Find the
        control that extends the bridge.

                    LUKE
        Oh, I think I just blasted it.

Luke looks at the blasted bridge control while the stormtroopers on
the opposite side of the door begin making ominous drilling and
pounding sounds.

                    LEIA
        They're coming through!

Luke notices something on his stormtrooper belt, when laserfire hits
the wall behind him. Luke aims his laser pistol at a stormtrooper
perched on a higher bridge overhang across the abyss from them. They
exchange fire. Two more troopers appear on another overhang, also
firing. A trooper is hit, and grabs at his chest.

Another trooper standing on a bridge overhang is hit by Luke's
laserfire, and plummets down the shaft. Troopers move back off the
bridge; Luke hands his gun to Leia.

                    LUKE
        Here, hold this.

Luke pulls a thin nylon cable from his trooper utility belt. It has
a grappler hook on it. A trooper appears on a bridge overhang and
fires at Luke and Leia. As Luke works with the rope, Leia returns
the laser volley. Another trooper appears and fires at them, as Leia
returns his fire as well. Suddenly, the hatch door begins to open,
revealing the feet of more troops.

                    LEIA
        Here they come!

Leia hits one of the stormtroopers on the bridge above, and he falls
into the abyss. Luke tosses the rope across the gorge and it wraps

CONTINUED:

itself around an outcropping of pipes. He tugs on the rope to make
sure it is secure, then grabs the princess in his arms. Leia looks
at Luke, then kisses him quickly on the lips. Luke is very
surprised.

                              LEIA
          For luck!

Luke pushes off and they swing across the treacherous abyss to the
corresponding hatchway on the opposite side. Just as Luke and Leia
reach the far side of the canyon, the stormtroopers break through
the hatch and begin to fire at the escaping duo. Luke returns the
fire before ducking into the tiny subhallway.

INT. DEATH STAR — NARROW PASSAGEWAY

Ben hides in the shadows of a narrow passageway as several
stormtroopers rush past him in the main hallway. He checks to make
sure they're gone, then runs down the hallway in the opposite direction. Darth Vader appears at the far end of the hallway and starts
after the old Jedi.

INT. DEATH STAR — MAIN FORWARD BAY

Threepio looks around at the troops milling about the pirateship
entry ramp.

                              THREEPIO
          Where could they be?

Artoo, plugged into the computer socket, turns his dome left and
right, beeping a response.

INT. DEATH STAR — CORRIDOR — BLAST SHIELD DOOR

Han and Chewbacca run down a long corridor with several troopers hot
on their trail.

                              TROOPER
          Close the blast doors!

At the end of the hallway, blast doors begin to close in front of
them. The young starpilot and his furry companion race past the huge
doors just as they are closing, and manage to get off a couple of
laserblasts at the pursuing troops before the doors slam shut.

                              TROOPER
          Open the blast doors! Open the blast doors!

INT. DEATH STAR — HALLWAY LEADING TO MAIN FORWARD BAY

Ben hurries along one of the tunnels leading to the hangar where the pirateship waits. Just before he reaches the hangar, Darth Vader steps into view at the end of the tunnel, not ten feet away. Vader lights his saber. Ben also ignites his and steps slowly forward.

> VADER
> I've been waiting for you, Obi-Wan. We meet again, at last. The circle is now complete.

Ben Kenobi moves with elegant ease into a classical offensive position. The fearsome Dark Knight takes a defensive stance.

> VADER
> When I left you, I was but the learner; now I am the master.

> BEN
> Only a master of evil, Darth.

The two Galactic warriors stand perfectly still for a few moments, sizing each other up and waiting for the right moment. Ben seems to be under increasing pressure and strain, as if an invisible weight were being placed upon him. He shakes his head and, blinking, tries to clear his eyes.

Ben makes a sudden lunge at the huge warrior but is checked by a lightning movement of the Sith. A masterful slash stroke by Vader is blocked by the old Jedi. Another of the Jedi's blows is blocked, then countered. Ben moves around the Dark Lord and starts backing into the massive starship hangar. The two powerful warriors stand motionless for a few moments with laser swords locked in midair, creating a low buzzing sound.

> VADER
> Your powers are weak, old man.

> BEN
> You can't win, Darth. If you strike me down, I shall become more powerful than you can possibly imagine.

Their lightsabers continue to meet in combat.

INT. DEATH STAR — MAIN FORWARD BAY

Han Solo and Chewbacca, their weapons in hand, lean back against the wall surveying the forward bay, watching the Imperial stormtroopers make their rounds of the hangar.

> HAN
> Didn't we just leave this party?

Chewbacca growls a reply, as Luke and the princess join them.

(CONTINUED)

CONTINUED:

                              HAN
          What kept you?

                              LEIA
          We ran into some old friends.

                              LUKE
          Is the ship all right?

                              HAN
          Seems okay, if we can get to it. Just hope
          the old man got the tractor beam out of
          commission.

INT. DEATH STAR — HALLWAY

Vader and Ben Kenobi continue their powerful duel. As they hit their
lightsabers together, lightning flashes on impact. Troopers look on
in interest as the old Jedi and Dark Lord of the Sith fight.
Suddenly Luke spots the battle from his group's vantage point.

                              LUKE
              Look!

Luke, Leia, Han, and Chewie look up and see Ben and Vader emerging
from the hallways on the far side of the docking bay.

INT. DEATH STAR — DOCKING BAY

Threepio and Artoo-Detoo are in the center of the Death Star's
Imperial docking bay.

                            THREEPIO
              Come on, Artoo, we're going!

Threepio ducks out of sight as the seven stormtroopers who were
guarding the starship rush past them heading toward Ben and the Sith
Knight. He pulls on Artoo.

INT. DEATH STAR — HALLWAY

Solo, Chewie, Luke, and Leia tensely watch the duel. The troops rush
toward the battling Knights.

                              HAN
                  Now's our chance! Go!

They start for the Millennium Falcon.

Ben sees the troops charging toward him and realizes that he is
trapped. Vader takes advantage of Ben's momentary distraction and

CONTINUED:

brings his mighty lightsaber down on the old man. Ben manages to deflect the blow and swiftly turns around.

The old Jedi Knight looks over his shoulder at Luke, lifts his sword from Vader's, then watches his opponent with a serene look on his face.

Vader brings his sword down, cutting old Ben in half. Ben's cloak falls to the floor in two parts, but Ben is not in it. Vader is puzzled at Ben's disappearance and pokes at the empty cloak. As the guards are distracted, the adventurers and the robots reach the starship. Luke sees Ben cut in two and starts for him. Aghast, he yells out.

                    LUKE
          No!

The stormtroopers turn toward Luke and begin firing at him. The robots are already moving up the ramp into the Millennium Falcon, while Luke, transfixed by anger and awe, returns their fire. Solo joins in the laserfire. Vader looks up and advances toward them, as one of his troopers is struck down.

                    HAN
          (to Luke) Come on!

                    LEIA
          Come on! Luke, it's too late!

                    HAN
          Blast the door! Kid!

Luke fires his laser pistol at the door control panel, and it explodes. The doors begin to slide shut. Three troopers charge forward firing laser bolts, as the door slides to a close behind them, shutting Vader and the other troops out of the docking bay. A stormtrooper lies dead at the feet of his onrushing compatriots. Luke starts for the advancing troops, as Solo and Leia move up the ramp into the pirateship. He fires, hitting a stormtrooper, who crumples to the floor.

                    BEN'S VOICE
          Run, Luke! Run!

Luke looks around to see where the voice came from. He turns toward the pirateship, ducking Imperial gunfire from the troopers and races into the ship.

INT. MILLENNIUM FALCON — COCKPIT

Han pulls back on the controls and the ship begins to move. The dull thud of laser bolts can be heard bouncing off the outside of the ship as Chewie adjusts his controls.

                                        (CONTINUED)

[94]

CONTINUED:

                          HAN
          I hope the old man got that tractor beam out
          of commission, or this is going to be a real
          short trip. Okay, hit it!

Chewbacca growls in agreement.

EXT. MILLENNIUM FALCON

The Millennium Falcon powers away from the Death Star docking bay,
makes a spectacular turn, and disappears into the vastness of space.

INT. MILLENNIUM FALCON — CENTRAL HOLD AREA

Luke, saddened by the loss of Obi-Wan Kenobi, stares off blankly as
the robots look on. Leia puts a blanket around him protectively, and
Luke turns and looks up at her. She sits down beside him.

INT. MILLENNIUM FALCON — COCKPIT

Solo spots approaching enemy ships.

                          HAN
          (to Chewie) We're coming up on their sentry
          ships. Hold 'em off! Angle the deflector
          shields while I charge up with the main guns!

INT. MILLENNIUM FALCON — CENTRAL HOLD AREA

Luke looks downward sadly, shaking his head back and forth, as the
princess smiles comfortingly at him.

                          LUKE
          I can't believe he's gone.

Artoo-Detoo beeps a reply.

                          LEIA
          There wasn't anything you could have done.

Han rushes into the hold area where Luke is sitting with the
princess.

                          HAN
          (to Luke) Come on, buddy, we're not out of
          this yet!

INT. MILLENNIUM FALCON — GUNPORTS — COCKPIT

Solo climbs into his attack position in the topside gunport.

INT. MILLENNIUM FALCON — HOLD AREA

Luke gets up and moves out toward the gunports as Leia heads for the cockpit.

INT. MILLENNIUM FALCON — GUNPORTS — COCKPIT

Luke climbs down the ladder into the gunport cockpit, settling into one of the two main laser cannons mounted in large rotating turrets on either side of the ship.

INT. MILLENNIUM FALCON — SOLO'S GUNPORT

Han adjusts his headset as he sits before the controls of his laser cannon, then speaks into the attached microphone.

                         HAN
          (to Luke) You in, kid? Okay, stay sharp!

INT. MILLENNIUM FALCON — GUNPORTS — COCKPIT

Chewbacca and Princess Leia search the heavens for the attacking TIE fighters. The Wookiee pulls back on the speed controls as the ship bounces slightly.

INT. MILLENNIUM FALCON — SOLO'S GUNPORT — COCKPIT

Computer graphic readouts form on Solo's target screen, as Han reaches for controls.

INT. MILLENNIUM FALCON — GUNPORT — COCKPIT

Luke sits in readiness for the attack, his hand on the laser cannon's control button.

INT. MILLENNIUM FALCON — COCKPIT

Chewbacca spots the enemy ships and barks.

(CONTINUED)

CONTINUED:

LEIA
(into intercom) Here they come!

INT. COCKPIT — POV (POINT OF VIEW) SPACE

The Imperial TIE fighters move toward the <u>Millennium Falcon</u>, one each veering off to the left and right of the pirateship.

INT. TIE FIGHTER — COCKPIT

The stars whip past behind the Imperial pilot as he adjusts his maneuvering joystick.

EXT. MILLENNIUM FALCON — IN SPACE

The TIE fighter races past the <u>Falcon</u>, firing laser beams as it passes.

INT. MILLENNIUM FALCON — HOLD AREA

Threepio is seated in the hold area, next to Artoo-Detoo. The pirateship bounces and vibrates as the power goes out in the room and then comes back on.

INT. MILLENNIUM FALCON — COCKPIT — GUNPORTS

A TIE fighter maneuvers in front of Han, who follows it and fires at it with the laser cannon. Luke does likewise, as the fighter streaks into view. The ship has suffered a minor hit, and bounces slightly.

EXT. SPACE

Two TIE fighters dive down toward the pirateship.

INT. MILLENNIUM FALCON — GUNPORTS

Luke fires at an unseen fighter.

LUKE
They're coming in too fast!

EXT. SPACE — MILLENNIUM FALCON/TIE FIGHTERS

Pan with pirateship as two TIE fighters charge through the
background. Laserbolts streak from all the craft.

INT. MILLENNIUM FALCON — CHEWBACCA

The ship shudders as a laserbolt hits very close to the cockpit. The
Wookiee chatters something to Leia.

EXT. TIE FIGHTER — SPACE

Full shot of a TIE fighter as it moves fast through the frame,
firing on the pirate starship.

EXT. SPACE — TIE FIGHTERS

The two TIE fighters fire a barrage of laserbeams at the pirateship.

INT. MILLENNIUM FALCON — MAIN PASSAGEWAY

A laserbolt streaks into the side of the pirateship. The ship
lurches violently, throwing poor Threepio into a cabinet full of
small computer chips.

                         THREEPIO
          Oooh!

INT. MILLENNIUM FALCON — COCKPIT GUNPORTS

Leia watches the computer readouts as Chewbacca manipulates the
ship's controls.

                         LEIA
          We've lost lateral controls.

                         HAN
          Don't worry, she'll hold together.

An enemy laserbolt hits the pirateship's control panel, causing it
to blow out in a shower of sparks.

                         HAN
          (to ship) You hear me, baby? Hold together!

Artoo-Detoo advances toward the smoking, sparking control panel,
dousing the inferno by spraying it with fire retardant, beeping all
the while.

INT. MILLENNIUM FALCON — GUNPORT

Luke swivels in his gun mount, following the TIE fighter with his laser cannon.

INT. MILLENNIUM FALCON — GUNPORT

Solo aims his laser cannon at the enemy fighters.

EXT. SPACE

A TIE fighter streaks in front of the starship.

INT. MILLENNIUM FALCON — COCKPIT

Leia watches the TIE ship fly over.

EXT. SPACE

A TIE fighter heads right for the pirateship, then zooms overhead.

INT. MILLENNIUM FALCON — GUNPORTS

Luke follows the TIE fighter across his field of view, firing laser-beams from his cannon.

EXT. TIE FIGHTER

A TIE fighter dives past the pirateship.

INT. MILLENNIUM FALCON — GUNPORTS

Luke fires at a TIE fighter. At his port, Han follows a fighter in his sights, releasing a blast of laserfire. He connects, and the fighter explodes into fiery dust. Han laughs victoriously.

EXT. SPACE

Two TIE fighters move toward and over the Millennium Falcon, unleashing a barrage of laserbolts at the ship.

INT. MILLENNIUM FALCON — GUNPORTS

Another TIE fighter moves in on the pirateship and Luke, smiling,
fires the laser cannon at it, scoring a spectacular direct hit.

                    LUKE
          Got him! I got him!

Han turns and gives Luke a victory wave, which Luke gleefully
returns.

                    HAN
          Great kid! Don't get cocky.

Han turns back to his laser cannon.

EXT. SPACE

Two more TIE fighters cross in front of the pirateship.

INT. MILLENNIUM FALCON — COCKPIT

While Chewbacca manipulates the controls, Leia turns, looking over
her shoulder out the ports.

                    LEIA
          There are still two more of them out there!

EXT. SPACE

A TIE fighter moves up over the pirateship, firing laserblasts
at it.

INT. MILLENNIUM FALCON — GUNPORTS

Luke and Han look into their respective projected target screens. An
Imperial fighter crosses Solo's port, and Han swivels in his chair,
following it with blasts from his laser cannon. Another fighter
crosses Luke's port, and he reacts in a like manner, the glow of his
target screen lighting his face.

EXT. SPACE

The TIE fighter zooms toward the pirateship, firing destructive
blasts at it.

INT. MILLENNIUM FALCON — GUNPORTS

Luke fires a laserblast at the approaching enemy fighter, and it
bursts into a spectacular explosion. Luke's projected screen gives a
readout of the hit. The pirateship bounces slightly as it is struck
by enemy fire.

EXT. SPACE — TIE FIGHTER

The last of the attacking Imperial TIE fighters looms in, firing
upon the Falcon.

INT. MILLENNIUM FALCON — GUNPORT

Solo swivels behind his laser cannon, his aim describing the arc of
the TIE fighter. The fighter comes closer, firing at the pirateship,
but a well-aimed blast from Solo's laser cannon hits the attacker,
which blows up in a small atomic shower of burning fragments.

                              LUKE
              (laughing) That's it! We did it!

The princess jumps up and gives Chewie a congratulatory hug.

                              LEIA
              We did it!

INT. MILLENNIUM FALCON — PASSAGEWAY

Threepio lies on the floor of the ship, completely tangled in the
smoking, sparking wires.

                            THREEPIO
              Help! I think I'm melting! (to Artoo) This is
              all your fault.

Artoo turns his dome from side to side, beeping in response.

EXT. SPACE — MILLENNIUM FALCON

The victorious Millennium Falcon moves off majestically through
space.

INT. DEATH STAR — CONTROL ROOM

Darth Vader strides into the control room, where Tarkin is watching
the huge viewscreen. A sea of stars is before him.

                                                    (CONTINUED)

CONTINUED:

                    TARKIN
        Are they away?

                    VADER
        They have just made the jump into hyperspace.

                    TARKIN
        You're sure the homing beacon is secure
        aboard their ship? I'm taking an awful risk,
        Vader. This had better work.

INT. MILLENNIUM FALCON — COCKPIT

Han, removing his gloves and smiling, is at the controls of the
ship. Chewie moves into the aft section to check the damage. Leia is
seated near Han.

                    HAN
        Not a bad bit of rescuing, huh? You know,
        sometimes I even amaze myself.

                    LEIA
        That doesn't sound too hard. Besides, they
        let us go. It's the only explanation for the
        ease of our escape.

                    HAN
        Easy . . . you call that easy?

                    LEIA
        They're tracking us!

                    HAN
        Not this ship, sister.

Frustrated, Leia shakes her head.

                    LEIA
        At least the information in Artoo is still
        intact.

                    HAN
        What's so important? What's he carrying?

                    LEIA
        The technical readouts of that battle
        station. I only hope that when the data is
        analyzed, a weakness can be found. It's not
        over yet!

                    HAN
        It is for me, sister! Look, I ain't in this
        for your revolution, and I'm not in it for
                    (MORE)

(CONTINUED)

CONTINUED:

                    HAN (CONT'D)
          you, Princess. I expect to be well paid. I'm
          in it for the money!

                    LEIA
          You needn't worry about your reward. If money
          is all that you love, then that's what you'll
          receive!

She angrily turns, and as she starts out of the cockpit, passes Luke
coming in.

                    LEIA
          Your friend is quite a mercenary. I wonder if
          he really cares about anything . . . or
          anybody.

                    LUKE
          I care!

Luke, shaking his head, sits in the copilot seat. He and Han stare
out at the vast blackness of space.

                    LUKE
          So . . . what do you think of her, Han?

                    HAN
          I'm trying not to, kid!

                    LUKE
          (under his breath) Good . . .

                    HAN
          Still, she's got a lot of spirit. I don't
          know, what do you think? Do you think a
          princess and a guy like me . . .

                    LUKE
          No!

Luke says it with finality and looks away. Han smiles at young
Luke's jealousy.

EXT. SPACE AROUND FOURTH MOON OF YAVIN

The battered pirateship drifts into orbit around the planet Yavin
and proceeds to one of its tiny green moons.

EXT. FOURTH MOON OF YAVIN

The pirateship soars over the dense jungle.

EXT. MASSASSI OUTPOST

An alert guard, his laser gun in hand, scans the countryside. He
sets the gun down and looks toward the temple, barely visible in the
foliage.

EXT. MASSASSI OUTPOST — JUNGLE TEMPLE

Rotting in a forest of gargantuan trees, an ancient temple lies
shrouded in an eerie mist. The air is heavy with the fantastic cries
of unimaginable creatures. Han, Luke, and the others are greeted by
the Rebel troops.

Luke and the group ride into the massive temple on an armored
military speeder.

INT. MASSASSI — MAIN HANGAR DECK

The military speeder stops in a huge spaceship hangar, set up in the
interior of the crumbling temple. Willard, the commander of the
Rebel forces, rushes up to the group and gives Leia a big hug.
Everyone is pleased to see her.

                    WILLARD
          (holding Leia) You're safe! We had feared the
          worst.

Willard composes himself, steps back, and bows formally.

                    WILLARD
          When we heard about Alderaan, we were afraid
          that you were . . . lost along with your
          father.

                    LEIA
          We don't have time for our sorrows,
          Commander. The battle station has surely
          tracked us here (looking pointedly at Han).
          It's the only explanation for the ease of our
          escape. You must use the information in this
          R2 unit to plan the attack. It is our only
          hope.

EXT. SPACE

The surface of the Death Star ominously approaches the red planet
Yavin.

INT. DEATH STAR - CONTROL ROOM

Grand Moff Tarkin and Lord Darth Vader are interrupted in their discussion by the buzz of the comlink. Tarkin moves to answer the call.

                    TARKIN
         Yes.

               DEATH STAR INTERCOM VOICE
         We are approaching the planet Yavin. The
         Rebel base is on a moon on the far side. We
         are preparing to orbit the planet.

EXT. YAVIN - JUNGLE

A lone guard stands in a tower high above the Yavin landscape, surveying the countryside. A mist hangs over the jungle of twisted green.

INT. MASSASSI - WAR ROOM BRIEFING AREA

Dodonna stands before a large electronic wall display. Leia and several other senators are to one side of the giant readout. The low-ceilinged room is filled with starpilots, navigators, and a sprinkling of R2-type robots. Everyone is listening intently to what Dodonna is saying. Han and Chewbacca are standing near the back.

                    DODONNA
         The battle station is heavily shielded and
         carries a firepower greater than half the
         starfleet. Its defenses are designed around a
         direct large-scale assault. A small one-man
         fighter should be able to penetrate the outer
         defense.

Gold Leader, a rough looking man in his early thirties, stands and addresses Dodonna.

                    GOLD LEADER
         Pardon me for asking, sir, but what good are
         snub fighters going to be against that?

                    DODONNA
         Well, the Empire doesn't consider a small
         one-man fighter to be any threat, or they'd
         have a tighter defense. An analysis of the
         plans provided by Princess Leia has demon-
         strated a weakness in the battle station.

(CONTINUED)

CONTINUED:

Artoo-Detoo stands next to a similar robot, makes beeping sounds, and turns his head from right to left.

                    DODONNA
          The approach will not be easy. You are
          required to maneuver straight down this
          trench and skim the surface to this point.
          The target area is only two meters wide. It's
          a small thermal exhaust port, right below the
          main port. The shaft leads directly to the
          reactor system. A precise hit will start a
          chain reaction which should destroy the
          station.

A murmur of disbelief runs through the room.

                    DODONNA
          Only a precise hit will set up a chain
          reaction. The shaft is ray-shielded, so
          you'll have to use proton torpedoes.

Luke is sitting next to Wedge Antilles, a hotshot pilot about sixteen years old.

                    WEDGE
          That's impossible, even for a computer.

                    LUKE
          It's not impossible. I used to bull's-eye
          womp rats in my T-sixteen back home. They're
          not much bigger than two meters.

                    DODONNA
          Man your ships! And may the Force be with
          you!

The group rises and begins to leave.

EXT. SPACE

The Death Star begins to move around the planet toward the tiny green moon.

INT. DEATH STAR

Tarkin and Vader watch the computer projected screen with interest, as a circle of lights intertwines around one another on the screen showing its position in relation to Yavin and the fourth moon.

                    DEATH STAR INTERCOM VOICE
          Orbiting the planet at maximum velocity. The
          moon with the Rebel base will be in range in
          thirty minutes.

CONTINUED:

                         VADER
          This will be a day long remembered. It has
          seen the end of Kenobi and will soon see the
          end of the Rebellion.

INT. MASSASSI OUTPOST — MAIN HANGAR DECK

Luke, Threepio, and little Artoo enter the huge spaceship hangar and
hurry along a long line of gleaming spacefighters. Flight crews rush
around loading last-minute armaments and unlocking power couplings.
In an area isolated from this activity Luke finds Han and Chewbacca
loading small boxes onto an armored speeder.

                     MAN'S VOICE
          (over loudspeaker) All flight troops, man
          your stations. All flight troops, man your
          stations.

Han is deliberately ignoring the activity of the fighter pilots'
preparations. Luke is quite saddened at the sight of his friend's
departure.

                         LUKE
          So . . . you got your reward and you're just
          leaving then?

                         HAN
          That's right, yeah! I got some old debts I've
          got to pay off with this stuff. Even if I
          didn't, you don't think I'd be fool enough to
          stick around here, do you? Why don't you come
          with us? You're pretty good in a fight. I
          could use you.

                         LUKE
          (getting angry) Come on! Why don't you take a
          look around? You know what's about to happen,
          what they're up against. They could use a
          good pilot like you. You're turning your back
          on them.

                         HAN
          What good's a reward if you ain't around to
          use it? Besides, attacking that battle
          station ain't my idea of courage. It's more
          like suicide.

                         LUKE
          All right. Well, take care of yourself, Han.
          I guess that's what you're best at, isn't it?

Luke goes off and Han hesitates, then calls to him.

                                                      (CONTINUED)

CONTINUED:

> HAN
> Hey, Luke . . . may the Force be with you!

Luke turns and sees Han wink at him. Luke lifts his hand in a small wave and then goes off.

Han turns to Chewie who growls at his captain.

> HAN
> What're you lookin' at? I know what I'm doing.

INT. MAIN HANGAR DECK — LUKE'S SHIP

Luke, Leia, and Dodonna meet under a huge spacefighter.

> LEIA
> What's wrong?

> LUKE
> Oh, it's Han! I don't know, I really thought he'd change his mind.

> LEIA
> He's got to follow his own path. No one can choose it for him.

> LUKE
> I only wish Ben were here.

Leia gives Luke a little kiss, turns, and goes off.

As Luke heads for his ship, another pilot rushes up to him and grabs his arm.

> BIGGS
> Luke! I don't believe it! How'd you get here . . . are you going out with us?!

> LUKE
> Biggs! Of course, I'll be up there with you! Listen, have I got some stories to tell you . . .

Red Leader, a rugged handsome man in his forties, comes up behind Luke and Biggs. He has the confident smile of a born leader.

> RED LEADER
> Are you . . . Luke Skywalker? Have you been checked out on the Incom T-sixty-five?

> BIGGS
> Sir, Luke is the best bushpilot in the outer rim territories.

(CONTINUED)

CONTINUED:

Pilot Leader pats Luke on the back as they stop in front of his fighter.

                    PILOT LEADER
          I met your father once when I was just a boy,
          he was a great pilot. You'll do all right. If
          you've got half of your father's skill,
          you'll do better than all right.

                    LUKE
          Thank you, sir. I'll try.

Red Leader hurries to his own ship.

                    BIGGS
          I've got to get aboard. Listen, you'll tell
          me your stories when we come back. All right?

                    LUKE
          I told you I'd make it someday, Biggs.

                    BIGGS
          (going off) You did, all right. It's going to
          be like old times, Luke. We're a couple of
          shooting stars that'll never be stopped!

Luke laughs and shakes his head in agreement. He heads for his ship.

As Luke begins to climb up the ladder into his sleek, deadly space-ship, the crew chief, who is working on the craft, points to little Artoo, who is being hoisted into a socket on the back of the fighter.

                    CHIEF
          This R2 unit of yours seems a bit beat up. Do
          you want a new one?

                    LUKE
          Not on your life! That little droid and I
          have been through a lot together. (to Artoo)
          You okay, Artoo?

The crewmen lower Artoo-Detoo into the craft. Now a part of the exterior shell of the starship, the little droid beeps that he is fine.

Luke climbs up into the cockpit of his fighter and puts on his helmet. Threepio looks on from the floor of the massive hangar as the crewmen secure his little electronic partner into Luke's X-wing. It's an emotion-filled moment as Artoo beeps good-bye.

                    CHIEF
          Okay, easy she goes!

                    THREEPIO
          Hang on tight, Artoo, you've got to come
          back.

                                        (CONTINUED)

CONTINUED:

Artoo beeps in agreement.

                    THREEPIO
          You wouldn't want my life to get boring,
          would you?

Artoo whistles his reply.

All final preparations are made for the approaching battle. The
hangar is buzzing with the last minute activity as the pilots and
crewmen alike make their final adjustments. The hum of activity is
occasionally trespassed by the distorted voice of the loudspeaker
issuing commands. Coupling hoses are disconnected from the ships as
they are fueled. Cockpit shields roll smoothly into place over each
pilot. A signalman, holding red guiding lights, directs the ships.
Luke, a trace of a smile gracing his lips, peers about through his
goggles.

                    BEN'S VOICE
          Luke, the Force will be with you.

Luke is confused at the voice and taps his headphones.

EXT. MASSASSI OUTPOST — JUNGLE

All that can be seen of the fortress is a lone guard standing on a
small pedestal jutting out above the dense jungle. The muted
gruesome crying sounds that naturally permeate this eerie purgatory
are overwhelmed by the thundering din of ion rockets as four silver
starships catapult from the foliage in a tight formation and disappear into the morning cloud cover.

INT. MASSASSI OUTPOST — WAR ROOM

The princess, Threepio, and a field commander sit quietly before the
giant display showing the planet Yavin and its four moons. The red
dot that represents the Death Star moves ever closer to the system.
A series of green dots appears around the fourth moon. A din of
indistinct chatter fills the war room.

                    MASSASSI INTERCOM VOICE
          Stand-by alert. Death Star approaching.
          Estimated time to firing range, fifteen
          minutes.

EXT. SPACE

The Death Star slowly moves behind the massive yellow surface of
Yavin in the foreground, as many X-wing fighters flying in formation
zoom toward us and out of the frame.

EXT. SPACE — ANOTHER ANGLE

Light from a distant sun creates an eerie atmospheric glow around a
huge planet, Yavin. Rebel fighters flying in formation settle
ominously in the foreground and very slowly pull away.

INT. RED LEADER STARSHIP — COCKPIT

Red Leader lowers his visor and adjusts his gun sights, looking to
each side at his wingmen.

                    RED LEADER
          All Wings report in.

INT. ANOTHER COCKPIT

One of the Rebel fighters checks in through his mike.

                    RED TEN
          Red Ten standing by.

INT. BIGGS'S COCKPIT

Biggs checks his fighter's controls, alert and ready for combat.

                    RED SEVEN
          (over Biggs's headset) Red Seven standing by.

                    BIGGS
          Red Three standing by.

INT. PORKINS'S COCKPIT

                    PORKINS
          Red Six standing by.

                    RED NINE
          (over headset) Red Nine standing by.

INT. WEDGE'S FIGHTER — COCKPIT

                    WEDGE
          Red Two standing by.

INT. LUKE'S X-WING FIGHTER — COCKPIT

                    RED ELEVEN
          (over headset) Red Eleven standing by.

                    LUKE
          Red Five standing by.

EXT. LUKE'S X-WING FIGHTER

Artoo-Detoo, in position outside of the fighter, turns his head from
side to side and makes beeping sounds.

INT. RED LEADER'S FIGHTER — COCKPIT

                    RED LEADER
          Lock S-foils in attack position.

EXT. SPACE

The group of X-wing fighters moves in formation toward the Death
Star, unfolding the wings and locking them into the "X" position.

INT. BIGGS'S COCKPIT

                    RED LEADER
          (over headset) We're passing through their
          magnetic field.

INT. RED LEADER'S COCKPIT

                    RED LEADER
          Hold tight!

INT. LUKE'S X-WING FIGHTER — COCKPIT

Luke adjusts his controls as he concentrates on the approaching
Death Star. The ship begins to be buffeted slightly.

                    RED LEADER
          (over headset) Switch your deflectors on.

INT. ANOTHER COCKPIT

                    RED LEADER
          (over headset) Double front!

EXT. SPACE

The fighters, now X-shaped darts, move in formation. The Death Star
now appears to be a small moon growing rapidly in size as the Rebel
fighters approach. Complex patterns on the metallic surface begin to
become visible. A large dish antenna is built into the surface on
one side.

INT. WEDGE'S COCKPIT

Wedge is amazed and slightly frightened at the awesome spectacle.

                    WEDGE
          Look at the size of that thing!

                    RED LEADER
          (over headset) Cut the chatter, Red Two.

INT. RED LEADER'S COCKPIT

                    RED LEADER
          Accelerate to attack speed. This is it, boys!

EXT. SPACE

As the fighters move closer to the Death Star, the awesome size of
the gargantuan Imperial fortress is revealed. Half of the deadly
space station is in shadow and this area sparkles with thousands of
small lights running in thin lines and occasionally grouped in large
clusters; somewhat like a city at night as seen from a weather
satellite.

INT. GOLD LEADER'S COCKPIT

                    GOLD LEADER
          Red Leader, this is Gold Leader.

                    RED LEADER
          (over headset) I copy, Gold Leader.

                    GOLD LEADER
          We're starting for the target shaft now.

INT. RED LEADER'S COCKPIT

Red Leader looks around at his wingmen, the Death Star looming in
from behind. Two Y-wing fighters bob back and forth in the
background. He moves his computer targeting device into position.

                    RED LEADER
          We're in position. I'm going to cut across
          the axis and try and draw their fire.

EXT. SPACE

Two squads of Rebel fighters peel off. The X-wings dive toward the
Death Star surface. A thousand lights glow across the dark gray
expanse of the huge station.

INT. DEATH STAR

Alarm sirens scream as soldiers scramble to large turbo-powered
laser gun emplacements. Electronic drivers rotate the huge guns into
position as the crew adjusts their targeting devices.

EXT. SPACE AROUND THE DEATH STAR

Laserbolts streak through the star-filled night. The Rebel X-wing
fighters move in toward the Imperial base, as the Death Star aims
its massive laser guns at the Rebel forces and fires.

INT. MASSASSI OUTPOST — WAR ROOM

Princess Leia listens to the battle over the intercom. Threepio is
at her side.

                    WEDGE
          (over war room speaker system) Heavy fire,
          boss! Twenty-three degrees.

                    RED LEADER
          (over speaker) I see it. Stay low.

EXT. SPACE

An X-wing zooms across the surface of the Death Star.

INT. DEATH STAR

Technical crews scurry here and there loading last-minute armaments and unlocking power cables.

INT. WEDGE'S COCKPIT

Wedge maneuvers his fighter toward the menacing Death Star.

EXT. SPACE

X-wings continue in their attack course on the Death Star.

INT. LUKE'S X-WING FIGHTER — COCKPIT

Luke nosedives radically, starting his attack on the monstrous fortress. The Death Star surface streaks past the cockpit window.

> LUKE
> This is Red Five; I'm going in!

EXT. SPACE

Luke's X-wing races toward the Death Star. Laserbolts streak from Luke's weapons, creating a huge fireball explosion on the dim surface.

INT. LUKE'S X-WING FIGHTER — COCKPIT

Terror crosses Luke's face as he realizes he won't be able to pull out in time to avoid the fireball.

> BIGGS
> (over headset) Luke, pull out!

EXT. SURFACE OF DEATH STAR

Luke's ship emerges from the fireball, with the leading edges of his wings slightly scorched.

INT. BIGGS'S COCKPIT

> BIGGS
> Are you all right?

INT. LUKE'S X-WING FIGHTER — COCKPIT

Luke adjusts his controls and breathes a sigh of relief. Flak bursts outside the cockpit window.

                              LUKE
               I got a little cooked, but I'm okay.

EXT. SURFACE OF THE DEATH STAR

Rebel fighters continue to strafe the Death Star's surface with laserbolts.

INT. DEATH STAR

Walls buckle and cave in. Troops and equipment are blown in all directions. Stormtroopers stagger out of the rubble. Standing in the middle of the chaos, a vision of calm and foreboding, is Darth Vader. One of his astro-officers rushes up to him.

                        ASTRO-OFFICER
               We count thirty Rebel ships, Lord Vader. But
               they're so small they're evading our
               turbo-lasers!

                             VADER
               We'll have to destroy them ship to ship. Get
               the crews to their fighters.

INT. DEATH STAR

Smoke belches from the giant laser guns as they wind up their turbine generators to create sufficient power. The crew rushes about preparing for another blast. Even the troopers' head gear is not adequate to protect them from the overwhelming noise of the monstrous weapon. One trooper bangs his helmet with his hand in an attempt to stop the ringing.

INT. RED LEADER'S X-WING — COCKPIT — TRAVELING

Red Leader flies through a heavy hail of flak.

                        RED LEADER
               Luke, let me know when you're going in.

INT. LUKE'S X-WING — COCKPIT — TRAVELING

The Red Leader's X-wing flies past Luke as he puts his nose down and
starts his attack dive.

                    LUKE
          I'm on my way in now . . .

                    RED LEADER
          Watch yourself! There's a lot of fire coming
          from the right side of that deflection tower.

                    LUKE
          I'm on it.

EXT. SURFACE OF THE DEATH STAR

Luke flings his X-wing into a twisting dive across the horizons and
down onto the dim gray surface.

EXT. LUKE'S X-WING — TRAVELING

A shot hurls from Luke's guns. Laserbolts streak toward the onrushing Death Star surface. Several small radar emplacements erupt in
flame. Laserfire erupts from a protruding tower on the surface.

INT. LUKE'S X-WING — COCKPIT — TRAVELING

The blurry Death Star surface races past the cockpit window as a big
smile sweeps across Luke's face at the success of his run. Flak
thunders on all sides of him.

EXT. SURFACE OF THE DEATH STAR

The Death Star superstructure races past Luke as he maneuvers his
craft through a wall of laserfire and peels away from the surface
toward the heavens.

INT. DEATH STAR

The thunder and smoke of the big guns reverberate throughout the
massive structure. Many soldiers rush about in the smoke and chaos,
silhouetted by the almost continual flash of explosions.

INT. BIGGS'S COCKPIT — TRAVELING

Biggs dives through a forest of radar domes, antennae, and gun
towers as he shoots low across the Death Star surface. A dense
barrage of laserfire streaks by on all sides.

INT. DEATH STAR

Imperial starpilots dash in unison to a line of small auxiliary
hatches that lead to Imperial TIE fighters.

INT. MASSASSI OUTPOST — WAR ROOM

Princess Leia, surrounded by her generals and aides, paces nervously
before a lighted computer table. On all sides technicians work in
front of many lighted glass walls. Dodonna watches quietly from one
corner. One of the officers working over a screen speaks into his
headset.

                    CONTROL OFFICER
          Squad leaders, we've picked up a new group of
          signals. Enemy fighters coming your way.

INT. LUKE'S X-WING FIGHTER — COCKPIT — TRAVELING

Luke looks around to see if he can spot the approaching Imperial
fighter.

                         LUKE
          My scope's negative. I don't see anything.

INT. RED LEADER'S X-WING — COCKPIT — TRAVELING

The Death Star's surface sweeps past as Red Leader searches the sky
for the Imperial fighter. Flak pounds at his ship.

                       RED LEADER
          Keep up your visual scanning. With all this
          jamming, they'll be on top of you before your
          scope can pick them up.

EXT. SURFACE OF THE DEATH STAR

Silhouetted against the rim lights of the Death Star horizon, four
ferocious Imperial TIE ships dive on the Rebel fighters. Two of the

                                                      (CONTINUED)

CONTINUED:

TIE fighters peel off and drop out of frame. Pan with the remaining two TIE ships.

INT. BIGGS'S COCKPIT — TRAVELING

Biggs panics when he discovers a TIE ship on his tail. The horizon in the background twists around as he peels off, hoping to lose the Imperial fighter.

INT. RED LEADER'S COCKPIT

                    RED LEADER
          Biggs! You've picked one up . . . watch it!

                      BIGGS
          I can't see it! Where is he?!

EXT. SPACE AROUND THE DEATH STAR

Biggs zooms off the surface and into space, closely followed by an Imperial TIE fighter. The TIE ship fires several laserbolts at Biggs, but misses.

INT. BIGGS'S COCKPIT — TRAVELING

Biggs sees the TIE ship behind him and swings around, trying to avoid him.

                      BIGGS
          He's on me tight, I can't shake him . . . I
          can't shake him.

EXT. SPACE AROUND THE DEATH STAR

Biggs, flying at high altitude, peels off and dives toward the Death Star surface, but he is unable to lose the TIE fighter, who sticks close to his tail.

INT. X-WING FIGHTER — COCKPIT — TRAVELING

Luke is flying upside down. He rotates his ship around to a normal attitude as he comes out of his dive.

                      LUKE
          Hang on, Biggs, I'm coming in.

EXT. SPACE AROUND THE DEATH STAR

Biggs and the tailing TIE ship dive for the surface, now followed by a fast-gaining Luke. After Biggs dives out of sight, Luke chases the Imperial fighter.

EXT. SURFACE OF THE DEATH STAR

In the foreground, the Imperial fighter races across the Death Star's surface, closely followed by Luke in the background.

INT. LUKE'S X-WING FIGHTER — COCKPIT — TRAVELING

There is a shot from Luke's X-wing of the TIE ship exploding in a mass of flames.

                         LUKE
          Got him!

INT. DEATH STAR

Darth Vader strides purposefully down a Death Star corridor, flanked by Imperial stormtroopers.

                         VADER
          Several fighters have broken off from the
          main group. Come with me!

INT. MASSASSI OUTPOST — WAR ROOM

A concerned Princess Leia, Threepio, Dodonna, and other officers of the Rebellion stand around the huge round readout screen, listening to the ship-to-ship communication on the room's loudspeaker.

                         BIGGS
          (over speaker) Pull in! Luke . . . pull in!

                         WEDGE
          (over speaker) Watch your back, Luke!

INT. LUKE'S X-WING FIGHTER — COCKPIT

                         WEDGE
          (over headset) Watch your back! Fighter's
          above you, coming in!

EXT. SPACE

Luke's ship soars away from the Death Star's surface as he spots the
tailing TIE fighter.

INT. TIE FIGHTER'S COCKPIT

The TIE pilot takes aim at Luke's X-wing.

EXT. SPACE

The Imperial TIE fighter pilot scores a hit on Luke's ship. Fire
breaks out on the right side of the X-wing.

INT. LUKE'S X-WING FIGHTER — COCKPIT

Luke looks out of his cockpit at the flames on his ship.
                              LUKE
                    I'm hit, but not bad.

EXT. LUKE'S X-WING FIGHTER

Smoke pours out from behind Artoo-Detoo.
                          LUKE'S VOICE
                    Artoo, see what you can do with it. Hang on
                    back there.
Green laserfire moves past the beeping little robot as his head
turns.

INT. LUKE'S X-WING — COCKPIT

Luke nervously works his controls.
                          RED LEADER
                    (over headset) Red Six . . .

INT. MASSASSI OUTPOST — WAR ROOM

In the war room, Leia stands frozen as she listens and worries
about Luke.
                          RED LEADER
                    (over speaker) Can you see Red Five?

(CONTINUED)

CONTINUED:

                         RED TEN
          (over speaker) There's a heavy fire zone on
          this side. Red Five, where are you?

INT. LUKE'S X-WING — COCKPIT

Luke spots the TIE fighters behind him and soars away from the Death
Star surface.

                         LUKE
          I can't shake him!

EXT. SURFACE OF THE DEATH STAR

Luke's ship soars closer to the surface of the Death Star, an
Imperial TIE fighter closing in on him in hot pursuit.

INT. WEDGE'S COCKPIT

The Death Star whips below Wedge.

                         WEDGE
          I'm on him, Luke!

INT. LUKE'S X-WING — COCKPIT

                         WEDGE
          (over headset) Hold on!

EXT. SURFACE OF THE DEATH STAR

Wedge dives across the horizon toward Luke and the TIE fighter.

INT. WEDGE'S COCKPIT

Wedge moves his X-wing in rapidly.

INT. LUKE'S X-WING — COCKPIT

Luke reacts frantically.

                         LUKE
          Blast it! Wedge, where are you?

INT. TIE FIGHTER — COCKPIT

The fighter pilot watches Wedge's X-wing approach. Another X-wing joins him, and both unleash a volley of laserfire on the Imperial fighter.

EXT. SPACE

The TIE fighter explodes, filling the screen with white light. Luke's ship can be seen far in the distance.

INT. LUKE'S X-WING — COCKPIT

Luke looks about in relief.

                         LUKE
          Thanks, Wedge.

INT. MASSASSI OUTPOST — WAR ROOM

Leia, Threepio, Dodonna, and other Rebel officers are listening to the Rebel fighter's radio transmissions over the war room intercom.
                         BIGGS
          (over speaker) Good shooting, Wedge!
                       GOLD LEADER
          (over speaker) Red Leader . . .

INT. GOLD LEADER'S Y-WING — COCKPIT

Gold Leader peels off and starts toward the long trenches at the Death Star surface pole.
                       GOLD LEADER
          . . . This is Gold Leader. We're starting our
          attack run.

EXT. SPACE AROUND THE DEATH STAR

Three Y-wing fighters of the Gold group dive out of the stars toward the Death Star surface.

INT. MASSASSI OUTPOST — WAR ROOM

Leia and the others are grouped around the screen, as technicians move about attending to their duties.

                                              (CONTINUED)

CONTINUED:

RED LEADER
(over speaker): I copy, Gold Leader. Move
into position.

EXT. SPACE AROUND THE DEATH STAR

Three Imperial TIE ships in precise formation dive toward the Death
Star surface.

INT. DARTH VADER'S COCKPIT

Darth Vader calmly adjusts his control stick as the stars whip past
in the window above his head.

VADER
Stay in attack formation!

INT. MASSASSI OUTPOST — WAR ROOM

Technicians are seated at the computer readout table.

GOLD LEADER
(over speaker) The exhaust port is . . .

INT. GOLD LEADER'S Y-WING — COCKPIT.

GOLD LEADER
. . . marked and locked in!

EXT. SPACE AROUND THE DEATH STAR

Gold Leader approaches the surface and pulls out to skim the surface
of the huge station. The ship moves into a deep trench, firing
laserbolts. The surface streaks past as laserfire is returned by the
Death Star.

INT. GOLD FIVE'S Y-WING — COCKPIT — TRAVELING

Gold Five is a pilot in his early fifties with a very battered
helmet that looks like it's been through many battles. He looks
around to see if enemy ships are near. His fighter is buffeted by
Imperial flak.

INT. GOLD LEADER'S Y-WING — COCKPIT

Gold Leader races down the enormous trench that leads to the exhaust port. Laserbolts blast toward him in increasing numbers, occasionally exploding near the ship causing it to bounce about.

                    GOLD LEADER
          Switch power to front deflector screens.

EXT. SURFACE OF THE DEATH STAR

Three Y-wings skim the Death Star surface deep in the trench, as laserbolts streak past on all sides.

EXT. DEATH STAR SURFACE — GUN EMPLACEMENT

An exterior surface gun blazes away at the oncoming Rebel fighters.

INT. GOLD LEADER'S Y-WING — COCKPIT

                    GOLD LEADER
          How many guns do you think, Gold Five?

INT. MASSASSI OUTPOST — WAR ROOM

                    GOLD FIVE
          (over speaker) I'd say about twenty guns.
          Some on the surface, some on the towers.

Leia, Threepio, and the technicians view the projected target screen, as red and blue target lights glow. The red target light near the center blinks on and off.

                    MASSASSI INTERCOM VOICE
          (over speaker) Death Star will be in range in
          five minutes.

EXT. SURFACE OF THE DEATH STAR

The three Y-wing fighters race toward camera and zoom overhead through a hail of laserfire.

INT. GOLD LEADER'S Y-WING — COCKPIT

Gold Leader pulls his computer targeting device down in front of his eye. Laserbolts continue to batter the Rebel craft.

                                        (CONTINUED)

CONTINUED:

> GOLD LEADER
> Switch to targeting computer.

INT. GOLD TWO'S Y-WING — COCKPIT

Gold Two, a younger pilot about Luke's age, pulls down his targeting
eye viewer and adjusts it. His ship shudders under intense laser
barrage.

> GOLD TWO
> Computer's locked. Getting a signal.

As the fighters begin to approach the target area, suddenly all the
laserfire stops. An eerie calm clings over the trench as the surface
whips past in a blur.

> GOLD TWO
> The guns . . . they've stopped!

EXT. SURFACE OF THE DEATH STAR

Two Y-wings zoom down the Death Star trench.

INT. GOLD FIVE'S COCKPIT

Gold Five looks behind him.

> GOLD FIVE
> Stabilize your rear deflectors. Watch for
> enemy fighters.

INT. GOLD LEADER'S Y-WING — COCKPIT

> GOLD LEADER
> They're coming in! Three marks at two ten.

EXT. SPACE AROUND THE DEATH STAR

Three Imperial TIE ships, Darth Vader in the center flanked by two
wingmen, dive in precise formation almost vertically toward the
Death Star surface.

INT. DARTH VADER'S COCKPIT

Darth Vader calmly adjusts his control stick as the stars zoom by.

(CONTINUED)

CONTINUED:

                          VADER
          I'll take them myself! Cover me!

                     WINGMAN'S VOICE
          (over speaker) Yes, sir.

EXT. SPACE AROUND THE DEATH STAR SURFACE

Three TIE fighters zoom across the surface of the Death Star.

INT. DARTH VADER'S COCKPIT

Vader lines up Gold Two in his targeting computer. Vader's hands
grip the control stick as he presses the button.

INT. GOLD TWO'S Y-WING — COCKPIT

The cockpit explodes around Gold Two. His head falls forward.

EXT. SPACE AROUND THE DEATH STAR

As Gold Two's ship explodes, debris is flung out into space.

INT. GOLD LEADER'S Y-WING — COCKPIT

Gold Leader looks over his shoulder at the scene.

INT. DEATH STAR TRENCH

The three TIE fighters race along in the trench in a tight
formation.

INT. GOLD LEADER'S Y-WING — COCKPIT

Gold Leader panics.

                         GOLD LEADER
          (into mike) I can't maneuver!

INT. GOLD FIVE'S Y-WING — COCKPIT

Gold Five, the old veteran, trys to calm Gold Leader.

                                                    (CONTINUED)

CONTINUED:

                         GOLD FIVE
          Stay on target.

INT. GOLD LEADER'S Y-WING — COCKPIT

The Death Star races by outside the cockpit window as he adjusts his
targeting device.

                         GOLD LEADER
               We're too close.

INT. GOLD FIVE'S Y-WING — COCKPIT

The older pilot remains calm.

                         GOLD FIVE
               Stay on target!

INT. GOLD LEADER'S Y-WING — COCKPIT

Now he's really panicked.

                         GOLD LEADER
               Loosen up!

INT. DARTH VADER'S COCKPIT

Vader calmly adjusts his targeting computer and pushes the fire
button.

INT. GOLD LEADER'S Y-WING — COCKPIT

Gold Leader's ship is hit by Vader's lasers.

EXT. SURFACE OF THE DEATH STAR

Gold Leader explodes in a ball of flames, throwing debris in all
directions.

INT. GOLD FIVE'S Y-WING — COCKPIT

Gold Five moves in on the exhaust port.

                         GOLD FIVE
                 Gold Five to Red Leader . . .

INT. LUKE'S X-WING FIGHTER — COCKPIT

Luke looks over his shoulder at the action outside of his cockpit.

                    GOLD FIVE
          (over headset) Lost Tiree, lost Dutch.

INT. RED LEADER'S COCKPIT

                    RED LEADER
          I copy, Gold Five.

INT. GOLD FIVE'S Y-WING — COCKPIT

                    GOLD FIVE
          They came from behind. . . .

EXT. SURFACE OF THE DEATH STAR

One of the engines explodes on Gold Five's Y-wing fighter, blazing
out of control. He dives past the horizon toward the Death Star's
surface, passing a TIE fighter during his descent. Gold Five, a
veteran of countless campaigns, spins toward his death.

INT. LUKE'S X-WING FIGHTER — COCKPIT

Luke looks nervously about him at the explosive battle.

INT. DEATH STAR — CONTROL ROOM

Grand Moff Tarkin and a chief officer stand in the Death Star's
control room.

                    OFFICER
          We've analyzed their attack, sir, and there
          is a danger. Should I have your ship standing
          by?

                    TARKIN
          Evacuate? In our moment of triumph? I think
          you overestimate their chances!

Tarkin turns to the computer readout screen. Flames move around the
green disk at the center of the screen, as numbers read across the
bottom.

                                             (CONTINUED)

[129]

CONTINUED:

                              VOICE
                    (over speaker) Rebel base, three minutes and
                    closing.

INT. RED LEADER'S COCKPIT

Red Leader looks over at his wingmen.

                              RED LEADER
                    Red Group, this is Red Leader.

INT. MASSASSI OUTPOST — WAR ROOM

Dodonna moves to the intercom as he fiddles with the computer keys.

                              RED LEADER
                    (over speaker) Rendezvous at mark six point
                    one.

                              WEDGE
                    (over speaker) This is Red Two. Flying toward
                    you.

                              BIGGS
                    (over speaker) Red Three, standing by.

INT. RED LEADER'S COCKPIT

                              DODONNA
                    (over headset) Red Leader, this is Base One.
                    Keep half your group out of range for the
                    next run.

INT. LUKE'S X-WING FIGHTER — COCKPIT

                              RED LEADER'S VOICE
                    (over headset) Copy, Base One. Luke, take Red
                    Two and Three. Hold up here and wait for my
                    signal . . . to start your run.

Luke nods his head.

EXT. SPACE AROUND THE DEATH STAR

The X-wing fighters of Luke, Biggs, and Wedge fly in formation high
above the Death Star's surface.

INT. LUKE'S X-WING FIGHTER — COCKPIT

Luke peers out from his cockpit.

EXT. SURFACE OF THE DEATH STAR

Two X-wings move across the surface of the Death Star. Red Leader's
X-wing drops down to the surface leading to the exhaust port.

INT. RED LEADER'S COCKPIT

Red Leader looks around to watch for the TIE fighters. He begins to
perspire.

                         RED LEADER
              This is it!

EXT. SPACE

Red Leader roams down the trench of the Death Star as lasers streak
across the black heavens.

EXT. DEATH STAR SURFACE — GUN EMPLACEMENT

A huge remote-control laser cannon fires at the approaching Rebel
fighters.

EXT. DEATH STAR TRENCH

The Rebel fighters evade the Imperial laserblasts.

INT. RED TEN'S COCKPIT

Red Ten looks around for the Imperial fighters.

                         RED TEN
              We should be able to see it by now.

EXT. DEATH STAR TRENCH

From the cockpits of the Rebel pilots, the surface of the Death Star
streaks by, with Imperial laserfire shooting toward them.

INT. RED LEADER'S COCKPIT

                    RED LEADER
          Keep your eyes open for those fighters!

INT. RED TEN'S COCKPIT

                    RED TEN
          There's too much interference!

EXT. SPACE — DEATH STAR TRENCH

Three X-wing fighters move in formation down the Death Star trench.
                    RED TEN'S VOICE
          Red Five, can you see them from where you
          are?

INT. LUKE'S X-WING FIGHTER — COCKPIT

Luke looks down at the Death Star surface below.

                    LUKE
          No sign of any . . . wait!

INT. RED TEN'S COCKPIT

Red Ten looks up and sees the Imperial fighters.

                    LUKE
          (over headset) Coming in point three five.

                    RED TEN
          I see them.

EXT. SURFACE OF THE DEATH STAR

Three TIE fighters, Vader flanked by two wingmen, dive in a tight
formation. The sun reflects off their dominate solar fins as they
loop toward the Death Star's surface.

INT. RED LEADER'S COCKPIT

Red Leader pulls his targeting device in front of his eyes and makes
several adjustments.

                                              (CONTINUED)

CONTINUED:

                         RED LEADER
          I'm in range.

EXT. SURFACE OF THE DEATH STAR

Red Leader's X-wing moves up the Death Star trench.

INT. RED LEADER'S COCKPIT

                         RED LEADER
               Target's coming up!

Red Leader looks at his computer target readout screen. He then
looks into his targeting device.

                         RED LEADER
               Just hold them off for a few seconds.

INT. DARTH VADER'S COCKPIT

Vader adjusts his control lever and dives on the X-wing fighters.

                         VADER
               Close up formation.

INT. DEATH STAR TRENCH

The three TIE fighters move in formation across the Death Star
surface.

INT. RED LEADER'S COCKPIT

                         RED LEADER
               Almost there!

Red Leader lines up his target on the targeting device crosshairs.

EXT. SURFACE OF THE DEATH STAR

Vader and his wingmen zoom down the trench.

INT. DARTH VADER'S COCKPIT

Vader rapidly approaches the two X-wings of Red Ten and Red Twelve.

(CONTINUED)

CONTINUED:

Vader's laser cannon flashes below the view of the front porthole.
The X-wings show in the center of Vader's computer screen.

EXT. SPACE

Red Twelve's X-wing fighter is hit by Vader's laserfire, and it
explodes into flames against the trench.

INT. RED TEN'S COCKPIT

Red Ten works at his controls furiously, trying to avoid Vader's
fighter behind him.

                    RED TEN
          You'd better let her loose.

INT. RED LEADER'S COCKPIT

Red Leader is concentrating on his targeting device.
                    RED LEADER
          Almost there!

INT. RED TEN'S COCKPIT

Red Ten panics.

                    RED TEN
          I can't hold them!

EXT. SURFACE OF THE DEATH STAR

Vader and his wingmen whip through the trench in pursuit of the
Rebel fighters.

INT. DARTH VADER'S COCKPIT

Vader coolly pushes the fire button on his control stick.

INT. RED TEN'S COCKPIT

Darth Vader's well-aimed laserfire proves to be unavoidable, and
strikes Red Ten's ship. Red Ten screams in anguish and pain.

EXT. SPACE AROUND THE DEATH STAR

Red Ten's ship explodes and bursts into flames.

INT. RED LEADER'S COCKPIT

Grimly, Red Leader takes careful aim and watches his computer targeting device, which shows the target lined up in the crosshairs, and fires.

INT. RED LEADER'S COCKPIT

                         RED LEADER
        It's away!

EXT. DEATH STAR SURFACE

Red Leader's X-wing pulls up just before a huge explosion billows out of the trench.

INT. DEATH STAR

An armed Imperial stormtrooper is knocked to the floor from the attack explosion. Other troopers scurrying about the corridors are knocked against the wall and lose their balance.

INT. MASSASSI OUTPOST — WAR ROOM

Leia and the others stare at the computer screen.
                      RED NINE'S VOICE
         (over speaker) It's a hit!

                         RED LEADER
         (over speaker) Negative.

INT. RED LEADER'S COCKPIT

Red Leader looks back at the receding Death Star. Tiny explosions are visible in the distance.
                         RED LEADER
          Negative! It didn't go in. It just impacted
          on the surface.

EXT. SPACE AROUND THE DEATH STAR — TIE FIGHTER

Darth Vader peels off in pursuit as Red Leader's X-wing passes the
Death Star horizon.

INT. DARTH VADER'S COCKPIT

Vader swings his ship around for his next kill.

INT. RED LEADER'S COCKPIT

                         LUKE
             (over headset) Red Leader, we're right above
             you. Turn to point . . .

INT. LUKE'S X-WING FIGHTER — COCKPIT

Luke tries to spot Red Leader. He looks down at the Death Star
surface.

                         LUKE
             . . . oh-five; we'll cover for you.

                       RED LEADER
             (over headset) Stay there . . .

INT. RED LEADER'S COCKPIT

A wary Red Leader looks about nervously.

                       RED LEADER
             . . . I just lost my starboard engine.

INT. LUKE'S X-WING FIGHTER — COCKPIT

Luke looks excitedly toward Red Leader's X-wing.

                       RED LEADER
             (over headset) Get set up for your attack
             run.

INT. DARTH VADER'S COCKPIT

Vader's gloved hands make contact with the control sticks, and he
presses their firing buttons.

INT. RED LEADER'S COCKPIT

Red Leader fights to gain control of his ship.

EXT. SPACE AROUND THE DEATH STAR

Laserbolts are flung from Vader's TIE fighter, connecting with Red
Leader's Rebel X-wing fighter. Red Leader buys it, creating a
tremendous explosion far below. He screams and is destroyed.

INT. LUKE'S X-WING FIGHTER — COCKPIT

Luke looks out the window of his X-wing at the explosion far below.
For the first time, he feels the helplessness of his situation.

INT. DEATH STAR

Grand Moff Tarkin casts a sinister eye at the computer screen.

                    DEATH STAR INTERCOM VOICE
              Rebel base, one minute and closing.

INT. MASSASSI OUTPOST — WAR ROOM

Dodonna and Princess Leia, with Threepio beside them, listen
intently to the talk between the pilots. The room is grim after Red
Leader's death. Princess Leia nervously paces the room.

                         LUKE
              (over speaker) Biggs, Wedge, let's close it
              up. We're going in. We're going in full
              throttle.

INT. WEDGE'S COCKPIT

The horizon twists as Wedge begins to pull out.

                         WEDGE
              Right with you, boss.

EXT. SPACE AROUND THE DEATH STAR

The two X-wings peel off against a background of stars and dive
toward the Death Star.

INT. BIGGS'S COCKPIT

> > > BIGGS
> > Luke, at that speed will you be able to pull
> > out in time?

INT. LUKE'S X-WING FIGHTER — COCKPIT

> > > LUKE
> > It'll be just like Beggar's Canyon back home.

EXT. SPACE AROUND THE DEATH STAR

The three X-wings move in, unleashing a barrage of laserfire. Laserbolts are returned from the Death Star.

INT. BIGGS'S COCKPIT

Luke's lifelong friend struggles with his controls.

> > > BIGGS
> > We'll stay back far enough to cover you.

INT. LUKE'S COCKPIT

Flak and laserbolts flash outside Luke's cockpit window.

> > > WEDGE
> > (over headset) My scope shows the tower, but
> > I can't see the exhaust port! Are you sure
> > the computer can hit it?

EXT. DEATH STAR — GUN EMPLACEMENT

The Death Star laser cannon slowly rotates as it shoots laserbolts.

INT. LUKE'S X-WING FIGHTER — COCKPIT

Luke looks around for the Imperial TIE fighters. He thinks for a
moment and then moves his targeting device into position.

> > > LUKE
> > Watch yourself! Increase speed full throttle!

INT. WEDGE'S COCKPIT

Wedge looks excitedly about for any sign of the TIE fighters.

                         WEDGE
              What about that tower?

INT. LUKE'S X-WING FIGHTER — COCKPIT

                              LUKE
                   You worry about those fighters! I'll worry
                   about the tower!

EXT. DEATH STAR SURFACE

Luke's X-wing streaks through the trench, firing lasers.

INT. LUKE'S X-WING FIGHTER — COCKPIT

Luke breaks into a nervous sweat as the laserfire is returned,
nicking one of his wings close to the engine.

                              LUKE
                   (to Artoo) Artoo . . . that, that stabi-
                   lizer's broken loose again! See if you can't
                   lock it down!

EXT. LUKE'S X-WING FIGHTER

Artoo works to repair the damages. The canyon wall rushes by in the
background, making his delicate task seem even more precarious.

EXT. DEATH STAR

Two laser cannons are firing on the Rebel fighters.

INT. WEDGE'S COCKPIT

Wedge looks up and sees the TIE ships.

INT. LUKE'S X-WING FIGHTER — COCKPIT

Luke's targeting device marks off the distance to the target.

EXT. SPACE AROUND THE DEATH STAR

Vader and his wingmen zoom closer.

INT. DARTH VADER'S COCKPIT

Vader adjusts his controls and fires laserbolts at two X-wings
flying down the trench. He scores a direct hit on Wedge.

INT. MASSASSI OUTPOST — WAR ROOM

Leia and the others are grouped around the computer board.

                    WEDGE
          (over speaker) I'm hit! I can't stay with
          you.

                    LUKE
          (over speaker) Get clear, Wedge.

INT. LUKE'S X-WING FIGHTER — COCKPIT

                    LUKE
          You can't do any more good back there!

INT. WEDGE'S COCKPIT

                    WEDGE
          Sorry!

EXT. SPACE AROUND THE DEATH STAR

Wedge pulls his crippled X-wing back away from the battle.

INT. DARTH VADER'S COCKPIT

Vader watches the escape but issues a command to his wingmen.

                    VADER
          Let him go! Stay on the leader!

EXT. SPACE AROUND THE DEATH STAR

Luke's X-wing speeds down the trench; the three TIE fighters, still in perfect unbroken formation, tail close behind.

INT. BIGGS'S COCKPIT

Biggs looks around at the TIE fighters. He is worried.
                         BIGGS
          Hurry, Luke, they're coming in much faster
          this time. I can't hold them!

EXT. SPACE AROUND THE DEATH STAR

The three TIE fighters move ever closer, closing in on Luke and Biggs.

INT. LUKE'S X-WING FIGHTER — COCKPIT

Luke looks back anxiously at little Artoo.
                         LUKE
          Artoo, try and increase the power!

EXT. LUKE'S X-WING FIGHTER

Ignoring the bumpy ride, flak, and lasers, a beeping Artoo-Detoo struggles to increase the power, his dome turning from side to side.

EXT. SPACE AROUND THE DEATH STAR

Stealthily, the TIE formation creeps closer.

INT. DARTH VADER'S COCKPIT

Vader adjusts his control stick.

INT. BIGGS'S COCKPIT

Biggs looks around at the TIE fighters.

INT. LUKE'S X-WING FIGHTER — COCKPIT

Luke looks into his targeting device. He moves it away for a moment
and ponders its use. He looks back into the computer targeter.

                              BIGGS
                (over headset) Hurry up, Luke!

EXT. SPACE AROUND THE DEATH STAR

Vader and his wingmen race through the Death Star trench. Biggs
moves in to cover for Luke, but Vader gains on him.

INT. BIGGS'S COCKPIT

Biggs sees the TIE fighters aiming at him.
                              BIGGS
            Wait!

INT. DARTH VADER'S COCKPIT

Vader squeezes the fire button on his controls.

INT. BIGGS'S COCKPIT

Biggs's cockpit explodes around him, lighting him in red.

EXT. SURFACE OF THE DEATH STAR

Biggs's ship bursts into a million flaming bits and scatters across
the surface.

INT. MASSASSI OUTPOST — WAR ROOM

Leia and the others stare at the computer board.

INT. LUKE'S X-WING COCKPIT

Luke is stunned by Biggs's death. His eyes are watering, but his
anger is also growing.

INT. DEATH STAR — CONTROL ROOM

Grand Moff Tarkin watches the projected target screen with
satisfaction.

                    DEATH STAR INTERCOM VOICE
            Rebel base, thirty seconds and closing.

INT. DARTH VADER'S COCKPIT

Vader takes aim on Luke and talks to his wingman.

                              VADER
                I'm on the leader.

EXT. SURFACE OF THE DEATH STAR — LUKE'S SHIP

Luke's ship streaks through the trench of the Death Star.

INT. MASSASSI OUTPOST — WAR ROOM

Princess Leia returns her general's worried and doubtful glances
with a solid, grim determination. Threepio seems nervous.

                            THREEPIO
                Hang on, Artoo!

INT. LUKE'S X-WING — COCKPIT

Luke concentrates on his targeting device.

EXT. SURFACE OF THE DEATH STAR

Three TIE fighters charge away down the trench toward Luke.

INT. DARTH VADER'S COCKPIT

Vader's fingers curl around the control stick.

INT. LUKE'S X-WING — COCKPIT

Luke adjusts the lens of his targeting device.

EXT. SURFACE OF THE DEATH STAR

Luke's ship charges down the trench.

INT. LUKE'S X-WING — COCKPIT

Luke lines up the yellow crosshair lines of the targeting device's
screen. He looks into the targeting device, then starts at a voice
he hears.

                          BEN'S VOICE
                    Use the Force, Luke.

EXT. SURFACE OF THE DEATH STAR

The Death Star trench zooms by.

INT. LUKE'S X-WING — COCKPIT

Luke looks up, then starts to look back into the targeting device.
He has second thoughts.
                          BEN'S VOICE
                    Let go, Luke.
A grim determination sweeps across Luke's face as he closes his eyes
and starts to mumble Ben's training to himself.

EXT. SURFACE OF THE DEATH STAR

Luke's fighter streaks through the trench.

INT. DARTH VADER'S COCKPIT

                            VADER
                  The Force is strong with this one!

EXT. SURFACE OF THE DEATH STAR

Vader follows Luke's X-wing down the trench.

INT. LUKE'S X-WING — COCKPIT

Luke looks to the targeting device, then away as he hears Ben's
voice.

                                                    (CONTINUED)

CONTINUED:

                    BEN'S VOICE
        Luke, trust me.

Luke's hand reaches for the control panel and presses the button.
The targeting device moves away.

INT. MASSASSI OUTPOST — WAR ROOM

Leia and the others stand watching the projected screen.

                    BASE VOICE
        (over speaker) His computer's off. Luke, you
        switched off your targeting computer. What's
        wrong?

                    LUKE
        (over speaker) Nothing. I'm all right.

EXT. SURFACE OF THE DEATH STAR

Luke's ship streaks ever closer to the exhaust port.

INT. LUKE'S X-WING — COCKPIT

Luke looks at the Death Star surface streaking by.

EXT. LUKE'S X-WING FIGHTER

Artoo-Detoo turns his head from side to side, beeping in
anticipation.

EXT. SURFACE OF THE DEATH STAR

The three TIE fighters, manned by Vader and his two wingmen, follow
Luke's X-wing down the trench.

INT. DARTH VADER'S COCKPIT

Vader maneuvers his controls as he looks at his doomed target. He
presses the fire buttons on his control sticks. Laserfire shoots
toward Luke's X-wing fighter.

EXT. LUKE'S X-WING FIGHTER

A large burst of Vader's laserfire engulfs Artoo. The arms go limp
on the smoking little droid as he makes a high-pitched sound.

INT. LUKE'S X-WING FIGHTER — COCKPIT

Luke looks frantically back over his shoulder at Artoo.

EXT. LUKE'S X-WING FIGHTER

Smoke billows out around little Artoo and sparks begin to fly.

                         LUKE
              I've lost Artoo!

Artoo's beeping sounds die out.

INT. MASSASSI OUTPOST — WAR ROOM

Leia and the others stare intently at the projected screen, while
Threepio watches the princess. Lights representing the Death Star
and targets glow brightly.

                    MASSASSI INTERCOM VOICE
              The Death Star has cleared the planet. The
              Death Star has cleared the planet.

INT. DEATH STAR — CONTROL ROOM

Tarkin glares at the projected target screen.

                    DEATH STAR INTERCOM VOICE
              Rebel base, in range.

                         TARKIN
              You may fire when ready.

                    DEATH STAR INTERCOM VOICE
              Commence primary ignition.

An officer reaches up and pushes buttons on the control panel, as
green lighted buttons turn to red.

EXT. SURFACE OF THE DEATH STAR

The three TIE fighters zoom down the Death Star trench in pursuit of
Luke, never breaking formation.

INT. LUKE'S COCKPIT

Luke looks anxiously at the exhaust port.

INT. DARTH VADER'S COCKPIT

Vader adjusts his control sticks, checking his projected targeting
screen.

EXT. SURFACE OF THE DEATH STAR

Luke's ship barrels down the trench.

INT. DARTH VADER'S COCKPIT

Vader's targeting computer swings around into position. Vader takes
careful aim on Luke's X-wing fighter.

                         VADER
          I have you now.

He pushes the fire buttons.

EXT. SURFACE OF THE DEATH STAR

The three TIE fighters move in on Luke. As Vader's center fighter
unleashes a volley of laserfire, one of the TIE ships at his side is
hit and explodes into flame. The two remaining ships continue to
move in.

INT. LUKE'S X-WING FIGHTER — COCKPIT

Luke looks about, wondering whose laserfire destroyed Vader's
wingman.

INT. DARTH VADER'S COCKPIT

Vader is taken by surprise, and looks out from his cockpit.

                         VADER
          What?

INT. DARTH VADER'S WINGMAN — COCKPIT

Vader's wingman searches around him trying to locate the unknown attacker.

INT. MILLENNIUM FALCON — COCKPIT

Han and Chewbacca grin from ear to ear.

                              HAN
               (yelling) Yahoo!

EXT. SPACE AROUND THE DEATH STAR

The Millennium Falcon heads right at the two TIE fighters. It's a collision course.

INT. WINGMAN'S COCKPIT

The wingman spots the pirateship coming at him and warns the Dark Lord.

                              WINGMAN
               Look out!

EXT. DEATH STAR TRENCH

Vader's wingman panics at the sight of the oncoming pirate starship and veers radically to one side, colliding with Vader's TIE fighter in the process. Vader's wingman crashes into the side wall of the trench and explodes. Vader's damaged ship spins out of the trench with a damaged wing.

EXT. SPACE AROUND THE DEATH STAR

Vader's ship spins out of control with a bent solar fin, heading for deep space.

INT. DARTH VADER'S COCKPIT

Vader turns round and round in circles as his ship spins into space.

EXT. SURFACE OF THE DEATH STAR

Solo's ship moves in toward the Death Star trench.

INT. MILLENNIUM FALCON — COCKPIT

Solo, smiling, speaks to Luke over his headset mike.

> HAN
> (into mike) You're all clear, kid.

INT. MASSASSI OUTPOST — WAR ROOM

Leia and the others listen to Solo's transmission.

> HAN
> (over speaker) Now let's blow this thing and
> go home!

INT. LUKE'S X-WING FIGHTER — COCKPIT

Luke looks up and smiles. He concentrates on the exhaust port, then
fires his laser torpedoes.

EXT. SURFACE OF THE DEATH STAR

Luke's torpedoes shoot toward the port and seem to simply disappear
into the surface and not explode. But the shots do find their mark
and have gone into the exhaust port and are heading for the main
reactor.

INT. LUKE'S X-WING FIGHTER — COCKPIT

Luke throws his head back in relief.

INT. DEATH STAR

An Imperial soldier runs to the control panel board and pulls the
attack lever as the board behind him lights up.

> INTERCOM VOICE
> Stand by to fire at Rebel base.

EXT. SPACE AROUND THE DEATH STAR

Two X-wings, a Y-wing, and the pirateship race toward Yavin in the distance.

INT. DEATH STAR

Several Imperial soldiers, flanking a pensive Grand Moff Tarkin, busily push control levers and buttons.

                         INTERCOM VOICE
          Standing by.

The rumble of a distant explosion begins.

EXT. SPACE AROUND THE DEATH STAR

The Rebel ships race out of sight, leaving the moon-like Death Star alone against a blanket of stars. Several small flashes appear on the surface. The Death Star bursts into a supernova, creating a spectacular heavenly display.

INT. MILLENNIUM FALCON — COCKPIT

                         HAN
          Great shot, kid. That was one in a million.

INT. LUKE'S X-WING FIGHTER — COCKPIT

Luke is at last at ease, and his eyes are closed.

                         BEN'S VOICE
          Remember, the Force will be with you . . .
          always.

The ship rocks back and forth.

EXT. DARTH VADER'S TIE FIGHTER

Vader's ship spins off into space.

EXT. SPACE

The Rebel ships race toward the fourth moon of Yavin.

INT. MASSASSI OUTPOST — MAIN HANGAR

Luke climbs out of his starship fighter and is cheered by a throng
of ground crew and pilots. Luke climbs down the ladder as they all
welcome him with laughter, cheers, and shouting.

Princess Leia rushes toward him.

                         LEIA
          Luke! Luke! Luke!

She throws her arms around Luke and hugs him as they dance around in
a circle. Solo runs in toward Luke and they embrace one another,
slapping each other on the back.

                         HAN
          (laughing) Hey! Hey!

                         LUKE
          (laughing) I knew you'd come back! I just
          knew it!

                         HAN
          Well, I wasn't gonna let you get all the
          credit and take all the reward.

Luke and Han look at one another, as Solo playfully shoves at Luke's
face. Leia moves in between them.

                         LEIA
          (laughing) Hey, I knew there was more to you
          than money.

Luke looks toward the ship.

                         LUKE
          Oh, no!

The fried little Artoo-Detoo is lifted off the back of the fighter
and carried off under the worried eyes of Threepio.

                         THREEPIO
          Oh, my! Artoo! Can you hear me? Say something!
          (to mechanic) You can repair him, can't you?

                         TECHNICIAN
          We'll get to work on him right away.

                         THREEPIO
          You must repair him! Sir, if any of my
          circuits or gears will help, I'll gladly
          donate them.

                         LUKE
          He'll be all right.

INT. MASSASSI OUTPOST — MAIN THRONE ROOM

Luke, Han, and Chewbacca enter the huge ruins of the main temple. Hundreds of troops are lined up in neat rows. Banners are flying and at the far end stands a vision in white, the beautiful young Senator Leia. Luke and the others solemnly march up the long aisle and kneel before Senator Leia. From one side of the temple marches a shined-up and fully repaired Artoo-Detoo. He waddles up to the group and stands next to an equally pristine Threepio, who is rather awestruck by the whole event. Chewbacca is confused. Dodonna and several other dignitaries sit on the left of Princess Leia. Leia is dressed in a long white dress and is staggeringly beautiful. She rises and places a gold medallion around Han's neck. He winks at her. She then repeats the ceremony with Luke, who is moved by the event. They turn and face the assembled troops, who all bow before them. Chewbacca growls and Artoo beeps with happiness.

FADE OUT

END CREDITS OVER STARS

THE END